Resist and Persist

Resist and Persist

Faith and the Fight for Equality

ERIN WATHEN

WESTMINSTER
JOHN KNOX PRESS
LOUISVILLE · KENTUCKY

First edition
Published by Westminster John Knox Press
Louisville, Kentucky

18 19 20 21 22 23 24 25 26 27—10 9 8 7 6 5 4 3 2 1

Book design by Drew Stevens
Cover design by Mark Abrams

Library of Congress Cataloging-in-Publication Data

Names: Wathen, Erin, author.
Title: Resist and persist : faith and the fight for equality / Erin Wathen.
Description: Louisville, KY : Westminster John Knox Press, 2018. |
    Identifiers: LCCN 2017050171 (print) | LCCN 2017052141 (ebook) | ISBN
    9781611648577 (ebk.) | ISBN 9780664263904 (pbk. : alk. paper)
Subjects: LCSH: Sex role—Religious aspects—Christianity. |
    Sexism—Religious aspects—Christianity. | Women—Religious
    aspects—Christianity. | Misogyny—Religious aspects—Christianity.
Classification: LCC BT708 (ebook) | LCC BT708 .W355 2018 (print) | DDC
    277.308/3082—dc23
LC record available at https://lccn.loc.gov/2017050171

Most Westminster John Knox Press books are available at special quantity discounts when purchased in bulk by corporations, organizations, and special-interest groups. For more information, please e-mail SpecialSales@wjkbooks.com.

With love and gratitude for all the fiery, fierce, and fabulous church ladies in my life: past, present, and future. I have known and loved many, and the world needs more of them, more than ever.

Contents

Introduction

Whenever I sit in my favorite coffee place, writing and people watching, I am constantly struck by people's shoes. Not in a philosophical, "where they've been" or "the things they've seen" kind of way, but by the fact that the men walking to work at the courthouse are wearing sensible, presumably comfortable loafers. Shoes that don't wreck your knees and ankles, distort your posture, and generally make you daydream all day about being barefoot.

On the other hand, the women walking to work at the courthouse are mostly wearing stylish instruments of torture. Because this is what we're told strikes the right balance of sex appeal and professionalism to earn us a seat at the table. Sure, fifty years ago we didn't get to come to the table at all—unless we were pouring the coffee. Nowadays, women make up nearly half of the U.S. workforce, but equal pay—not to mention representation in higher executive positions—is still far off. According to the letter of the law, we have every right to be there. But the subtext of our highly gendered culture says we can achieve that equal status only by adhering to the laws of the boys' club—and, of course, its highwire act of a dress code for women.

We need a new language for feminism, because misogyny looks a lot different than it did a few decades ago. In some ways, we've moved beyond the days of overt ass-grabbing, telling the "little woman" she doesn't belong in the workplace, and having no representation in government and other places of power.

And yet . . . in many ways it's the same story for a different day. The ass-grabbing is much more subtle and indirect. It's in rape culture and microaggressions. It's in the shoes we are expected to wear, the dress codes that don't apply to our male colleagues, and the unspoken pressures of juggling motherhood with professional life. Or the pressure to be a mother at all, when perhaps that is not our calling. In many ways, sexism has only gotten more brash and repulsive as women have gained power and voice in the mainstream culture. The patriarchy dies hard; it has to find new and artful ways to function in the civilized world, and those new ways are often even uglier than the old ones.

Misogyny for the modern age is in watching the first major-party female presidential candidate get heckled off the political stage. After a lifetime of public service, she was ultimately painted as shrill, unlikable, and "crooked," criticized and vilified for doing what men in her position have done, and still do, forever and ever, amen.

We are in the age of double standards and impossible expectations; a never-die patriarchy that is sanctioned by every institution: capitalism, government, and even—maybe especially—the church itself.

But for all this, many women still don't recognize the real impact this system has on their lives. They do not identify as feminists, they feel this is "not their fight," and in many ways they even perpetuate the systems that continue to harm women. Meanwhile, many men who care about, affirm, and empower women do not call themselves feminists—because they cannot see or acknowledge the privilege granted to them by nature and anatomy.

Maybe, for the new expressions of misogyny present in our time and place, the language of traditional feminism fails us. It is time for a new lexicon of female empowerment; a more compassionate and nuanced conversation; a movement that can be inclusive of all women, regardless of age, race, religion, or economic status.

We need to change the conversation. For a new generation of feminists who have more opportunity than our mothers and grandmothers ever dreamed of—and for all the women who have never felt they had a place in this fight. For women of color who have been marginalized even in the fight for equality. For Millennial women who find the language of feminism off-putting and archaic. For conservative women who shut down any further discussion the minute the word "abortion" comes up. We need a much bigger table to host all of these voices, to hear all of these stories. Because we all still live in the same world, which is, in so many ways, a man's world. We still find ourselves glancing over our shoulders at night, rolling our eyes in board meetings, and wondering if we will ever be "enough" for our families, for our employers, for the world.

This cannot be the plight of just the middle-aged white woman. The work of equality must include women of every age and ethnicity, as well as men who will be allies, advocates, and partners for the journey. But even more than that, if women are ever going to be fully free and equal in modern culture, it is going to take the voice of the church calling loudly for that equality. As one of the primary guardians—we might even say architects—of the patriarchy, the church must play a critical role in dismantling the language, the worldview, and the systems that tilt the tables in favor of men.

We have all been deeply conditioned to uphold "man's place" at the head of the table—whether that is the kitchen table, the boardroom table, or the communion table. These notions of male entitlement to leadership and power run deep, and they touch every institution that shapes our collective lives. This means the way forward is complicated. It bears implications for our family systems, our leadership structures, even our government life. In many cases, even women are reluctant to engage in the kind of paradigm shifts that it would take to bring about full equality for women. That means it will not be easy to draw the community of faith into the work of equality. But for this moment in our history, it is imperative that we do. The language and stories of our faith point to an ethic of justice, inclusion, and empowerment. Without women's voices fully heard, we cannot be faithful to that gospel calling. What follows is a conversation in the direction of change—by no means exhaustive, but by all means necessary. My hope is that communities of faith will find new ways to engage topics like rape culture, the wage gap, and yes, even reproductive health, in just and compassionate new ways, while creating a space for more voices in our midst, and at all of our many tables.

1

The Patriarchy Dies Hard

First, an airing of the grievances: I am a feminist because of the church. Because of one church in particular, actually.

That might sound strange enough, in and of itself. Adding some context will make it sound even stranger still; the church that raised me to be a feminist is located in a rural part of southeastern Kentucky.

Granted, it was a midsize, mainline church on Main Street, and not a one-room country meetinghouse. And my denomination, the Disciples of Christ, has been ordaining women since 1853, so I grew up never once hearing a Scripture referencing how women should be silent in churches. I saw women serving communion and praying at the table from the moment I was born. I occasionally heard a woman preach. I saw women teaching all levels of Sunday school, including adult classes that included (gasp!) grown-up men. I never once heard the word "feminist" uttered in that place, but every part of church life modeled to me that women had a place in leadership. It was never even a question.

When I was in high school and occasionally started bringing friends to worship or youth group activities with me, they thought it was so cool that there were women leading worship. "What do you mean?" I asked them with a completely straight sixteen-year-old face.

"Well, in my church, women can't stand up front," they'd tell me. "Women can't speak in worship, or pray aloud, or teach the men in Sunday school."

What? This was the first time such a stark reality of my own community was made known to me. But it was certainly not the last.

As the truth of Christian (and cultural) patriarchy began unfolding for me, I was outraged. Even before I knew the depths of how the church's ingrained misogyny touched every other part of public life, I was horrified that places existed where women's voices didn't matter. Where women were taught that their silence—and their never-cut hair—was their glory, their greatest asset. At the same time, I was filled with pride and gratitude that my own family of faith had somehow managed to raise me—and all the girls of our church—apart from those limitations, even within our own community and culture. For all of my young life, I was oblivious to the fact that women did not have equal voice and value in all worshiping communities. It is an extraordinary thing to grow up as a woman in that part of the world and never once question your voice, your place, your ability to lead and be a part of things.

To this day, I align that mixture of outrage and gratitude with the early stirrings of a call to ministry. My incredulous "What do you mean, women can't be ministers?" echoed with an unspoken but audible echo of "The hell I can't," and "You just watch me." That tension between thanksgiving and anger has served me well in this vocational life, and life in general. I am always mindful of the privilege of having been given voice at a young age, while also recognizing that not all girls have been afforded that same model. Heck, most girls in my own hometown were raised a world away, figuratively speaking.

But here's the sad part of the story, the grievance. In the end, it wasn't enough. The church that raised me, empowered me, and ordained me still failed the ultimate test of equality;

when it came right down to it, they would not call a woman to be their senior pastor.

She was the candidate chosen by the search committee, the leader who was clearly most qualified, who had a calling for the work—and even the community—and was willing to move to this small Kentucky town because she saw the Spirit at work in this particular congregation. She was The One.

I probably don't have to spell out the rest for you. There followed a textbook church conflict. Longtime inactive members and extended family members were called home for the vote—and ultimately, a margin of affirmation that was far too thin to secure the call.

A few years later, that beloved community left the denomination. Because like most mainline bodies, the Christian Church (Disciples of Christ) was becoming "too liberal" in regards to LGBT inclusion. But there was much more at work there than just a single hot-button issue. Having moved to a fearful place, an anxious place, that church I loved so well made a cliché of itself. Having caved to the cultural norms of the surrounding community—including the all-too-normal norm of patriarchy—they are no different now from every other church in that part of the world.

Rejecting a female leader was the first nod to its power; the rise of homophobia was the next natural unfolding. In these, and in so many other ways, the church—as we know it in the Western world—has been so powerfully shaped by the cultural norms of patriarchy that we don't always even know when we are in its grip.

CHURCH OF THE EMPIRE

Patriarchy in the church is nothing new. In fact, it is so deeply entrenched in the Christian narrative that it is difficult to parse out all the factors that led us to this place of systemic inequality. Some of our assumptions about power, gender, and worth are deeply rooted in our reading (and misreading) of Scripture.

But others have more to do with cultural, historical, and political influence along the way.

In the earliest days of the church, Christian communities were circles of peace and, often, resistance to the empire. As such, they were frequently persecuted, viewed as outliers and a threat to "law and order." During the early fourth century, though, Constantine saw an opportunity to harness the power of the church—which had continued to grow in spite of attempts to stifle it—to stabilize the crumbling Roman Empire. Over time, the relationship between church and empire made for some convoluted messaging. Under the influence of Constantine and his successors, that theology of peace and resistance evolved into a theology of dominance and control, intertwined with the power of the state.[1] Next thing you know, crosses—the symbol of torture, control, and the power of empire—began to appear as symbols of Christianity (supplanting the *ichthus* and *chi rho* as primary emblems of Jesus Christ), and the focus of faith turned from a resurrection theology of hope to a cross theology of fear, guilt, and control. Fast forward to the early days of America—God's "new Israel" some called it—where Christian domination of the continent was a widely accepted value, perhaps even a divine calling. It's no wonder that the young new nation came to worship, not the God of Israel, but the god of capitalism—which is itself the very idol of modern patriarchy.

It goes on like this, so that what we have now is a secular movement full of crosses, money, and masculinity. This modern movement worships power and follows material success, far more than it follows an itinerant peace-loving Jewish teacher. And so it happens that our contemporary expressions of church preserve the patriarchy. Both the American dream and the Western Christian narrative are powerfully entrenched in a worldview that holds a man's voice, role, and person as authoritative and values a woman primarily in terms of her connection with (and usefulness to) the men around her. Each of those institutions—the American capitalist dream and Western Christianity—work to uphold the inherent sexism of the other. For all the progress women have made in regards to rights by the letter of the law, living into an egalitarian ideal is slow going. Women have earned the right to vote and own property, to serve in the military, to pursue an education or any vocation of their choosing; and women are more financially independent than ever before. Yet, despite all these legal advances, we still live within systems that make it hard to realize full equality. Having rights is one thing. Seeing those rights put into practice across the board is another matter entirely.

It's an especially maddening time to be a woman, because we've come so far. Yet, in painful ways both large and small, we are still far from being fully equal members of society.

The 2016 election cycle brought this truth to light in some heartbreaking ways—and some maddening, outrageous ways. Politics aside, this goes way past party, or even candidate loyalty. The race for president was an ugly display of misogyny from the beginning. As it progressed, the leading candidate seemed to never suffer in the polls for his demeaning, degrading, and disregarding women. The barrage of overt sexism throughout the campaign seemed never-ending. Hillary Clinton, the first woman to ever get so close to the presidency, may not have been the perfect candidate. But rather than just *not voting for her*, much of America trolled her, hard, in a way that male candidates have never had to endure. She was criticized, loudly and crassly, for her looks; she was blamed for the sins of her husband; and she was vilified for political tactics that men in similar roles have used for centuries. Ultimately, the campaign of misogyny and fake news was enough to keep her out of power.

To many American women, that felt both global and personal.

At that point, it was not so much about who didn't win as it was about the sense that all women, everywhere, lost. We lost all the progress of the past few decades, and we lost the hope that we were going to be the generation to see full equality and representation in our lifetime.

For many of us, the disappointment was a rallying call to a new kind of activism. This isn't over. But clearly the traditional forms of feminism aren't working. So it's time for some changes in the dialogue among women and for changes in our institutional rhetoric as well.

For me, the election was an echo of my own story with my home church: moving along for years thinking you are in a place that is enlightened and inclusive—only to find, No! Wait! On second thought, women *are* better in the kitchen and behind the secretary's desk, and we're going to just keep right on letting these guys run things, because hey, neckties just make us feel more comfortable in some vague and indescribable way . . .

Yes, it's maddening. But it's becoming clear, now more than ever, that if we want to see real progress for women, the faith community is going to have to be a much bigger part of the conversation. We're going to have to find ways to actively engage the people in our circles—men and women alike, as well as our wider communities—in real solutions that make life better and more fair for women. While many of these issues may be loaded with political baggage, there are plenty of places to connect and work for change that should be not only bipartisan but also rooted in the gospel.

In spite of everything, 53 percent of white women voted for Trump, which shows how deeply we hold a shared acceptance of his misogynistic worldview. If we are passive in accepting this message, then we are complicit in upholding it for our daughters. Meanwhile, a gut-wrenching 81 percent of white evangelical Christians voted for him. To be clear, these votes were about more than the man himself, more than the "brand" he cultivated to reach the top of the ticket. This was a vote for a platform that promised to subvert the rights of women and minorities in the interest of preserving the patriarchy—not just the set of behaviors that implies but the status quo of an entire system that is geared toward preserving male power and diminishing that of women. While the margin of victory was narrow, it's clear that many who claim to follow Christ hold the values of that patriarchal world as a higher priority than those of the kingdom.

THIS IS EVERYONE'S BUSINESS

Nowadays, when someone tells me they aren't a feminist, I tilt my head and I raise an eyebrow. Everything else I know about this person tells me that they believe in equal pay; that they believe women to be capable of advancement in any field; and that they are against any expression of sexual aggression. How can anyone who believes in these basic truths *not* be a feminist? It's a matter of humanitarian necessity that women be recognized as full and equal partners with men in every context—from home and family to business and government. It is of great global and historical importance that we keep expanding this conversation and its partners to address all the new and evolving—not to mention ancient, preexisting—expressions of sexism. Yet too often, as much as it seems like a no-brainer to some of us, it appears that even those who recognize the need for equality do not see themselves as being connected to the work. If language is our only problem, then we should change the language. But my sense is that language is only part of the disconnect.

When someone says, "I'm not a feminist," one of a few things is usually true. Either (a) they do not believe that sexism still exists, and therefore feel there is no need for feminism; (b) they have a certain stereotype in mind about what it means to be a feminist, and they cannot make the stretch to write themselves into that narrative; or (c) they have so internalized the values of a patriarchal society, and those prescribed gender roles are so comfortable in their own lives, that they see no disconnect between the way things are and the way they could—or should—be. (We will further discuss this concept of "internalized misogyny" in chapter 2.) Therefore, they can't recognize the widespread and systemic injustices resulting for women worldwide, from abuse and objectification to poverty and human trafficking. Patriarchy remains hard at work to preserve itself, in all of these scenarios.

Many folks have the *Mad Men* kind of misogyny burned into their imaginations. When you mention sexism, they picture ass-grabbing, cigar-smoking, "Go get us some coffee, honey" kinds of normalized behavior. Admittedly, part of the charm of the acclaimed AMC drama is the retro vibe, a "remember those days" kind of sentimentality or even a self-congratulatory "look how far we've come" response. The danger there is that in our collective imagination we begin to see that world itself as retro—bygone days when women were treated with overt disregard by men who didn't know any better. Logging that part of our history into a category of bygones, however, allows us to think that we have evolved, that we are past the days of preferential treatment for men, and that other kinds of sexism haven't evolved to fill the void.

This is patently false.

In 2012 author Laura Bates took to Twitter with the #YesAllWomen hashtag to prove this very point. A spokeswoman for what many are calling Fourth Wave Feminism, Bates wanted to demonstrate the reality of pervasive sexist thinking and the kinds of abuse and harassment that thinking perpetuates. She asked women to tweet their experiences of being harassed or verbally abused, of being passed over for opportunities, or of having their voices diminished. The responses were overwhelming. The stories of women's personal experiences of harassment, discrimination, and assault confirm what statistics reveal about the frequency with which women meet male aggression: 87 percent of American women age eighteen to sixty-four have been harassed by a male stranger; and 41 percent of American women have experienced "physically aggressive" forms of harassment or assault in public spaces, including sexual touching, being followed, or being flashed.[2]

In her book *Everyday Sexism*, Bates shares many of these tweets, stitching together a visible mosaic of the ongoing aggressions to which women are subjected in the course of their day-to-day lives. Alongside those stories, she shares hard statistics about women's underrepresentation in nearly every part of public life. The connections between these sexist worldviews and opportunities for women are undeniable. Bates writes:

Women [in the United States] hold one-fifth or less of seats in the Senate and the House of Representatives. Only 35 women in history have ever served as governor, compared to more than 2300 men. Just four of the 112 justices ever to serve on the Supreme Court have been women. The *New York Times* reported in 2014 that women run a quarter of the biggest art museums in the United States, and earn about a third less than their male counterparts for doing so. Eighty percent of the reviewers and authors of reviewed books in the *New York Review of Books* in 2013 were men, as were almost 80 percent of the "notable deaths" reported in the *New York Times* in 2012. Data from the U.S. National Science Foundation reveals that women make up just 20 percent of architects, 17 percent of economists, and 11 percent of engineers. Only 5 percent of CEO's at Fortune 500 companies are women. The full-time pay gap is around 20 percent overall. Around one in five women in the United States has experienced rape or attempted rape at some time in her life, and more than one in three have experienced intimate partner violence. On average, more than three women every day are killed by a current or former partner.[3]

The statistics above apply *just* to women in the United States; they scarcely touch on the global plight of women. But as Bates also says, "Disbelief is the great silencer."[4] A commitment to ignorance, whether willful or otherwise, is the primary source of denial when it comes to people removing themselves from the conversation about gender and equality.

These statistics are several years old. The House of Representatives is now 19.3 percent female, while twenty-one of the 100 U.S. Senate seats are held by women.[5] That's not much improvement over the past few decades. And the whole women CEO thing *just* crept up from 5 to 6 percent in 2017. If we inch up by 1 percent every five years, then women will hold equal corporate power with men by roughly the year . . . well, never. At least, not in my lifetime. Probably not in your lifetime. Or our kids' lifetimes, for that matter. (Something like 200 years. Pardon me if I'm not jumping up and down about that.)

Do all women *want* to be CEOs or senators? Of course not. But that isn't the point. The point is that women who want to should be able to get there. As long as they don't have women role models, women's voices in the room, and women to be mentors and friends on the way up, it is a tedious uphill climb. Furthermore, as long as women have a minimal presence in rooms where decisions get made—whether it's the board room, the House of Representatives, or the Vatican—then the systems around which we order our lives are always going to be tilted in favor of men and men's interests.

The litany of abuse and underrepresentation demonstrated in the #YesAllWomen thread and in the everyday stories of every woman you know is just a surface argument for the ongoing work of equality—both why it is needed and why people of faith everywhere need to be involved in the conversation. This is not a job for only a secular, leftist, radical fringe of women. To fully realize the vision of a world that is fair and just for all, we need men at the table as well, and women of every generation and political persuasion, especially women of color, whose voices have been subverted for generations. The stories of women who have gone before us remind us how far we've come—but also how far there is yet to go.

It cannot be denied that the word "feminism" carries a lot of cultural baggage. Bra-burning, podium-thumping, man-hating, mascara-rejecting . . . am I getting close? There's a certain image that the F-word conjures up in the collective imaginations of many. While a certain brand of feminist may fit this prototype, it's unfortunate that the word has come to be so limiting for so many. Don't get me wrong; women who fit this angry and vocal model of feminism were (and are) more than entitled to their anger. But we should not assume that adopting this language, tone, and even wardrobe is a prerequisite for the work of equality.

We also can't overlook the fact that, for a great number of people living in our current context, the word "feminism" is synonymous with "abortion." While reproductive rights are a critical part of the discourse surrounding equality, one's views on that one matter should not preclude you from the conversation. Later in this book, in chapter 10, we'll explore what I hope is a more compassionate and nuanced approach to the issue, one that will bring more women (and men) to the table, regardless of their current stance or political persuasion.

Men and women alike have been deeply conditioned to accept a certain amount of male privilege as just the way things are. The same is true of deeply normalized gender roles. We just get used to the fact that most high-level executives are men, and that most commercials for cleaning products and minivans will feature women and women's lives. These are not isolated realities. They are profoundly connected. That women are the choosers of the toilet cleaner and that men are presiding over board meetings are two profoundly entwined cultural expectations, each relying on the other.

These deeply entrenched cultural norms are nearly impossible to overcome without intentional resistance and the cultivating of a counternarrative. Many view the crafting of that counternarrative as a divisive ideological issue—partly because of the inherent assumption that "feminist" is synonymous with "baby killer." But also because all of our societal systems work hard to uphold that measure of male superiority: academia, government, the sciences, Wall Street, Hollywood, and of course the church. Each of these institutions has been shaped by generations of male-dominated culture, and therefore established and upheld by men's voices, values, and vision. So, despite all the inroads women have made in each field, women are still functioning within the context of a cultural narrative created by and for men. The saying "It's a man's world" is cliché for a reason.

PART OF THE PROBLEM, PART OF THE SOLUTION

We cannot go back in time and unwind all the ways that the male perspective has shaped and formed the world we're living in now. What we can do is reject the notion that the institutions responsible for the long-standing tradition of patriarchy can't have a role in changing that tradition. We can also counter the assumption that the work of equality must, by definition, take place in an entirely secular frame. Just as those in the boardroom can change the assumptions about who is buying toilet cleaner, the church—the body of Christ, the global family of faith—can and must play a role in ending the daily atrocities enacted upon women worldwide. While most folks who participate in the life of an American Christian congregation will insist that they are not sexist—that women's voices are valued, and equal, even if sometimes found in different expressions of church life—the math speaks for itself.

Over the past decade, the number of female clergy in Protestant America has doubled, and roughly 10 percent of congregations have a woman in a primary leadership role. But when you start looking at churches of a certain *size*, the numbers have changed very little. While nearly half of all newly ordained clergy leaving seminary are women, there are still very few holding senior-pastor roles in larger congregations. And there remains a pay gap, to the tune of 27 percent, between female clergy and their male counterparts.[6]

Hard statistics aside, I can attest to this reality in purely anecdotal fashion. Many of my clergy sisters know for a fact that they are making less than their male predecessor at the same congregation. The sad truth is that as churches decrease in size and struggle to resource their ministry, they often call a female pastor because they think they can get away with paying her less. I know many women who have even had search committees say to them, outright, "Well, won't your husband be working too?" As though the existence of a husband and his inherent earning potential effectively diminish the value of her seminary degree and the skills she will bring to the position.

Don't do that, church. Just . . . don't. Not only is it completely asinine; it is against the dang law. I love congregations; I'd hate to see one of y'all get sued.

The happy news is this: sometimes when a church hires a female pastor—seemingly on the cheap—they get more than they bargained for. They find that her particular set of gifts and skills is uniquely suited for their congregation, in their particular time and place. They find there is untold growth potential in many parts of her being, her way of preaching and accompanying, her way of engaging leaders and challenging the status quo. They find that the brave spirit it often takes to call a woman in the first place leads the congregation itself to be transformed in exciting ways.

As a pastor myself, I spend a lot of time trolling other church's websites. While, yes, there are still traditions and parts of the country where a woman preacher is tantamount to a unicorn—as in, it doesn't exist/can't exist/would be a crime against nature if it did exist—I have a growing sense that, in most large churches and nearly all mainline churches, women as pastors are not strictly forbidden. They just aren't exactly celebrated or empowered.

Try this little experiment: Find a few midsize to large congregations in your community. Then go to the staff page of their website. You may find a few women there—likely as administrators and music leaders, at first! But you may also see some who are leading things called "community life" or "mission and outreach." You will certainly find them in children and youth ministry—possibly even with the job title of "children's pastor." You may even find clergy couples who are honored as the "pastors" of a church.

But dig a little deeper, and the line in the sand is around preaching. Women can be called, ordained, even employed, in many churches where they will never stand behind the microphone. Unless they are addressing a roomful of ladies (because I guess you have to have lady parts to be able to talk to an all-women gathering?). Where did the church get this idea that men can teach and lead both men and women, but women can speak only the language of women? Do we not see what an absurd disconnect that is? In fact, there are plenty of instances in Scripture where women are teaching and leading in many ways—from Mary and Martha to Lydia and Dorcas.

But, as Rachel Held Evans notes, "Unfortunately, when it comes to womanhood, many Christians tend to read the rest of Scripture through the lens of 1 Timothy 2:11–15 rather than the other way around."[7] Yes, there are a few texts in Scripture that indicate women should keep silent. But rather than viewing those through the wider lens of the biblical narrative as a whole, we've let those verses speak larger and louder than the rest of Scripture combined. As a result, women's voices have been limited, if not omitted altogether, throughout Christian history. But this was not always the case. One simple way that churches can engage the work of equality is to reject such a limited reading of Scripture. If teachers and preachers could approach those selective verses with a view of their place in the whole of the biblical narrative, we'd find that they were never intended to speak for all women across all time.

In the earliest days of the Christian church, women started out on equal footing with men. There was a time when the sentiment "there is no longer Jew nor Greek, . . . slave or free, . . . male and female; for all of you are one in Christ Jesus"[8] was the rule of the day. It was commonly accepted that once a believer entered into baptism, all boundaries of national identity, faith history, economic status, and even gender just fell away. All that mattered was identity in Christ and faithfulness to the mission and life in community.

Mary Magdalene, one of the few women mentioned by name multiple times in the Gospels, is one of the first to witness the resurrection and, as such, is the first preacher of the gospel and the first evangelist. Though not named as one of the twelve, she is clearly a "disciple," in the purest sense of the world: following, learning from, and serving alongside Jesus through thick and thin. Women held many positions of leadership in the early church. Many women were leaders of house churches, the first congregations; they served as deacons, evangelists, and servants of the gospel. Though we don't hear much of their story, we know some of their names: Appia, Nympha, Lydia, Chloe, Phoebe.

How did we get from there to banning women from the pulpit? It's the same thing experienced by many women throughout history in general and Scripture in particular. Their names get dropped from the credits. Their legacy was not enough to keep women empowered over the centuries. Over time, the church's radical and countercultural move toward egalitarianism was overridden by the wider male-dominated culture. The pressures and influences of his surroundings and his own history and experience colored Paul's reading of ancient texts.

Sexist as Paul may have been (simply by virtue of his culture, if nothing else), many scholars say that the verses specifically silencing women were likely penned not by Paul himself but by a later scribe writing commentary on that era. It bears resemblance to the second-century apostolic church—the days of the letters of Timothy and Titus, an era in which women's roles became severely diminished. Over time, and under the influence of the Constantine administration (as we mentioned before), translators like Jerome and those working for King James didn't have to work very hard to skew the Bible toward a total canon of masculine leadership. The male hierarchy was literally sanctified by the empire, making it nearly impossible to extract the original spirit of the Christian movement from the culture of which it was a product.

But the Scriptures most often used to silence/limit women have been dramatically "proof-texted," that is, lifted intentionally out of their entirety and context for the purpose of supporting a particular worldview. While these carefully selected texts might uphold, in some simplistic readings, a diminished voice for women, a more nuanced reading of Scripture shows that progressive, even radical-for-the-time views of women breathe throughout the Hebrew Bible, the Gospels, and the stories of the early church.

Jesus was a feminist.

The Jerry Falwell set are clutching their pearls right about now. But it's true.

Though perhaps not in the framework and expressions we would associate with women's rights in our own time, Jesus in many ways is an advocate for women's rights and fuller inclusion of women's voices in the spread of the gospel. For the time and place of his life and ministry, Jesus' voice is one of equality and inclusion. He frequently brings women into circles where others think they do not belong; includes them in the life of discipleship; heals and acknowledges and converses with them (to the horror, sometimes, of the other disciples); and ultimately recognizes the full humanity of women in a way that seems a bit radical in light of other cultural considerations of the time.

LOSING SIGHT OF THE GOSPEL'S
FOCUS ON INCLUSION

I'll tell you what I see in my own little corner of the world: nice suburban folks who prefer not to ask hard questions, who fully believe that women are equal to men in every way, but have no problem at all going to a church where women can do anything but preach. They just really never let that part of their lives intersect with everything else they believe and value.

If we believe in equality in the boardroom and the halls of Congress, we can't let the church off the hook. Despite our following an inclusive, feminist Messiah, the greater representation some churches are giving women in leadership is more a sign of secular and cultural progress than any real theological awakening across Westernized religion. That demonstrates the power, however imperfect, of the secular women's rights movement. Given our cultural, political, and biblical history, that we even got this far is a miracle. At the same time, just imagine what would happen if a faith-based women's movement took root within our tradition and joined forces with the secular work of equality. The transformation of the whole church, the community, even the world, would be astounding.

If its millennia-long complicity in a patriarchal, misogynistic system is not enough to call the modern church to action, then maybe its stake in the future will be. There are many reasons for people of faith to step into the fight for equality as never before, reasons that have nothing to do with ideology and everything to do with the values we claim to embody as followers of Christ and the biblical narrative that shapes the identity of believers.

Many of the most pressing justice issues of our time relate directly to the lack of women's voices in our shared power structures—from church to government to corporate America. These are matters the church is called to address directly:

— poverty
— racism
— access to health care
— family leave and healthy family life
— human trafficking
— sexual assault and domestic violence

Just to name a few. In the coming chapters we will explore how each of these social crises is rooted in the gender imbalance that shapes our global culture—particularly our American culture. In some cases, the connections to sexism are obvious; in others, the roots are more complex. But all of these issues have one thing in common: none of them should be partisan or controversial. They are not women's issues; they are humanitarian issues. They are systemic and societal issues that affect all of us—men and women alike. They all speak to conditions that directly counter God's creative vision for the world.

While approaching these issues from a uniquely womanist perspective may seem edgy at first in some settings, the church is in fact uniquely situated to address all of these complex conversations, bringing as many diverse voices as possible to the table and working deeply within communities to uproot our broken systems. While there's no way we're going to burn down this system, mine all of its history, and fix all the things in a day (or even in a single book), we can begin to unwind the ways in which our faith and culture are entwined with destructive ideas about women—and then begin to transform that unfortunate dynamic into something new, shifting the perception that feminism is some radical leftist agenda, understanding it instead as something hopeful and life-giving for all.

Far too many people still view the work of equality as elevating women at the expense of men, or insisting on a certain kind of vocational identity for all women, regardless of our individual gifts, callings, and worldviews. The emergence of absurd "men's rights groups" bears witness to this misconception, as does the cadre of antifeminist books and blogs *written by women*. It is far past time to shift this narrative, expressing a broader understanding of feminism as a worldview that elevates humanity as a whole.

It's time to gather up, lean in, and move forward. Maybe that means changing the language. Maybe that means changing the conversation. One thing is for sure: we are going to need everyone at the table.

Questions for Reflection and Discussion

1. What messages did you receive in your upbringing about what women's roles should be in the life of the faith community? For women: has that teaching affected how you approach other aspects of your life? For men: has that message affected how you engage with women in other aspects of your life?
2. Think of some strong women who were influential in your upbringing. Name what gifts they shared with you, and how they shaped your faith.
3. What images or words do you associate with the word "feminism"? If you have negative connotations, where do you think you learned those associations?

2
Other Women Are Not the Problem

They were the greatest of frenemies. Peggy and Joan. While Don Draper drank and womanized, destroyed his family, and dazzled the world of advertising from his corner office, the women of *Mad Men* created a world of their own. Their story line spoke for itself. Their plot lines expressed the lives of countless professional women; while proximity and circumstance invited them to be friends and allies, a deeper cultural influence often made them adversaries.

The backdrop of the advertising world made *Mad Men* the perfect show to explore the complex tensions between women, as women's roles and options changed dramatically throughout that period of history. The story of what it meant to be a woman played out in visible ways throughout the course of the show: in commercials, on billboards, and in women's magazine ads. That was an era in which the buying power of women became widely recognized across all industries, from big tobacco and big auto to household items and political candidates. Advertisers also realized the many ways in which a woman, whether or not she was directly making the purchase, might influence the decision of her husband or father.

As ads became increasingly geared toward women, those ads also began to define women—or rather, the parameters and expectations of what it meant to be a woman. In a single show, *Mad Men* was able to explore those messages through both the ads themselves and the women working behind the scenes to craft the messages. These women—first given responsibilities around only the "women's stuff," like lipstick and pantyhose and tampons—eventually found voice in all sorts of products and broader cultural conversations. At the same time, they lived into two very different narratives of femininity.

On the one hand, you have a Joan: strong, unflappable, and willing to use her sexuality to get ahead in the workplace. On the other hand you have a Peggy: young and hungry, though not yet comfortable in her own skin, "dressing like a child" (as Joan frequently reminds her), and—in spite of a rough start when it comes to the men in the office—determined that she will be recognized for her talent and brains and not reduced to her physical assets. Throughout the course of the show, the two women are constantly at odds with each other. Fundamentally, their conflict is about what it means to be a woman—not just in the professional world, but in the world at large.

Joan and Peggy (who, I frequently have to remind myself, are *fictional characters*) embody two interpretations of what it means to be a woman—each empowered, in her own way; each still coming up short, somehow, in the "man's world" she is forced to inhabit; and each sometimes resentful of the other for dealing with misogyny in a different way. Though they can be friends at times, each woman struggles to recognize the other as an equally legitimate expression of strong womanhood.

You don't have to be a faithful fan of the show to see how these two women represent two early waves of feminism. First Wave Feminism, spanning a period of history roughly covering 1848 to 1920, marks the long struggle during which U.S. women earned the right to vote. Second Wave Feminism kicks into high gear during the late 1960s, and carries through to the late 1980s. During this time, abortion is legalized, sexual freedoms are expanded with the evolution of the pill, and women earn (closer to) equal rights in the workplace. Women of this era literally invent the word "sexism," encourage each other to get an education and pursue careers, and identify violence against women as a visible crime.[1]

The world of *Mad Men* then drops us into the years running up to that momentous Second Wave, and by the end of the show the feminist thunder is in full force. Joan, being just a few years older than Peggy, is a daughter of the First Wave. She takes a head-down, get-along-to-get-ahead approach to her professional climb. While we in 2017 find it deeply problematic (to say the least) that she has to sleep with the Jaguar executive to be made partner, it is a brilliant story line to highlight the ways in which a woman's sexuality manifests as both strength and weakness while also exposing a deeply broken system in which the women of that era are so often cornered. Meanwhile Peggy—a glimpse ahead to the next wave of feminism—ends the show with roads wide open ahead of her. She comes into her own and reaches her professional goals on her own terms.

Neither of these characters is perfect, but each, in her own way, tells an important story about the changing lives of women in the 1960s.

Fast forward a few decades and we still live into this painful truth: that women are often pitted against each other in real-life, real-time kinds of ways, both professionally and otherwise. It may be that, like Joan and Peggy, we are living between waves of feminism, and that what empowered womanhood means to, say, a Gen Xer is not what it means to a Millennial—just as a Boomer feminist might disagree entirely with her granddaughter (or great granddaughter) from Generation Z. Expressions of womanhood are constantly evolving, as are the ways we coexist in that frame.

MORE THAN A FEW YEARS BETWEEN US

Despite generational tensions between women of different eras, we cannot reduce the systemic ways in which women are programmed to compete with each other. The memo conveyed by patriarchal culture, through everything from reproductive health policy to dress codes, is the suggestion that *women can't be trusted*, a damaging message internalized by many women as the belief that women cannot trust other women, that other women are the enemy with whom we must compete: for jobs, for men, for the vague approval of the patriarchy.

Need I point out that we ask women to compete in *actual beauty contests*? While acknowledging that I have friends for whom the pageant world has offered tremendous opportunity, those women also have talents and skills and academic prowess that have offered them far greater advancement. We use words like "opportunity" to justify a scenario in which women actually walk around on stage in a bikini and receive a grade—often from male judges. Gross. Pageant culture is not the issue, but, like so many expressions of patriarchy, it is certainly a symptom of the larger disease: the world of male-dominant values that makes an entertainment sport of women competing for the highest score.

Many argue that the contests are not sexist because the women are scored on other elements besides beauty, or that it's all fine because women are willing participants. But the bottom line is that there is no similar system built into our shared culture by which men jockey for the approval of female judges, based almost solely on their adherence to some narrow parameters of beauty and sexuality. Donald Trump, as owner of the Miss Universe pageant, forged much of his brand on the foundation of this world. It speaks volumes about U.S. culture's overarching view of women that this man got himself elected president.

The message is clear and simple: there is limited room at the table for women, so women have to compete for the few spots available. It's the classic scarcity mentality, repackaged for the gender wars. What we see in the dynamics between Peggy and Joan, on their worst days, is an expression of that tension. They each see something inherently threatening in the other's chosen definition of femininity. There is suspicion, competition, resentment, and ultimately some mistrust of the other.

That stuff runs deep. Even a woman who has deep, healthy friendships with other women may react viscerally to a woman who challenges her understanding and embodiment of womanhood. For instance, this is where we get "the mommy wars"—the ongoing tension between the women who choose to be full-time wives and mothers and the women with full-time vocational lives, who may or may not have kids at home. Decisions about breastfeeding, schools, screen time, organic food, and more add to the "mompetition" and self-doubt as we compare ourselves to other women.

Where on earth did we get the message that any of these choices makes us inherently more worthy of love and belonging, that either of these life paths will bring fullness of life, while the other is fundamentally flawed or lacking?

The worlds of capitalism and patriarchy have colluded to put us in these boxes and to make us feel as if we have to compete with each other—especially in the man's world, which doesn't really want us around to begin with. Powerful men perpetuate mistrust among women, because it is to their distinct advantage that strong women be at odds with each other.

Vice President Pence has revealed that his wife, Karen, serves as his "gut check and shield"[2] and that he makes it a point to never be alone with a woman other than his wife.[3] This practice echoes that of Billy Graham and other evangelical pastors who have employed such a policy as a sign of their commitment to sexual purity, avoidance of temptation, and fear of scandal that might damage their careers. Graham has long sent aides into hotel rooms before he enters, on the chance a woman and photographer are setting him up for a compromising photo.[4] We do not know the thoughts or motives of Mike and Karen Pence, but the rationale behind these policies overlooks the reality that it is *men* who often pose a physical threat to women and that many men should not be left alone in these scenarios. Not because women might come on to them, but because the men themselves are not responsible

enough with their own boundaries and the appropriate proto-
cols of social norms and personal space.

Women are ever mindful of all the places where we should
not go alone—like a secluded alley, or an office with a closed
door, or pretty much anywhere after dark. Do men recognize the imbalance here? Not likely. Because in their world,
the world of privileged white maleness, it's the women who
can't be trusted. The message of such a worldview is that we
should applaud a man who doesn't put himself in a situation
to be tempted by a woman. That we women should probably keep our own men on a short leash, because all these
other women out there are going to lure them into deep and
mortal sin. That women can't trust other women. Divide and
conquer. This narrative has enabled the patriarchy for centuries, compelling women themselves—even subconsciously—
to embrace the narrative that women are dirty whores and
home-wrecking trollops. So of course, if you are a man, you
should never be in a room with a woman other than your
spouse, because sex is the only obvious outcome. Or at least,
impure thoughts.

This view of women is dripping with male privilege. Do you
think that a woman could make it in the professional world if
she decided one day, "You know, I think I'm just not going
to ever put myself in a situation where I'm in a room alone
with a man." Talk to my best friend who's made a career in
the sciences. Ask her how far she'd go in that field if she tried
to sequester herself like that. Ask any of my female clergy colleagues the same. Or any woman in a top executive position.
Or in academia . . . the list goes on. The bottom line is that
there might be inherent risk in some of these situations, but the
risk is primarily the woman's. And often she has to take that
risk if she's going to "make it" in a man's world.

No, only a man could adopt such an absurd practice and
still find himself the vice president of the free world . . . because
he knows there are no women as gatekeepers between him and
where he wants to be.

And where does he want to be? How about: in a room where he is the tie-breaking vote on a major decision about women's healthcare. Where he can reject the voices of all the women in the room—even those from his own party—and still move to take away funding and provisions for women's health. Because women can't be trusted. Not to draft policy, and not to make decisions about their own bodies.

It may seem subtle, but it's not an accident.

This lack of regard for women as whole people—with worth beyond their sexual desirability and availability—is indefensible.

Here's what I wish Mike Pence knew: it's his loss if he avoids significant professional contact or friendships with women. He is missing out on meaningful connections. He's missing out on a wider worldview that would sure come in handy in his line of work. He's missing out on the wit and wisdom of his female colleagues, and all the ways that he might be made better by their support, all the ways they might push the edges of his thinking and challenge him to, God forbid, evolve.

As a woman, I'm grateful for the men in my life who know better. Male clergy colleagues who have ridden with me in cars on the way to long meetings and held space for my struggles in ministry. Guy friends who sit with me in restaurants, coffee shops, and bars all over this country—scandalously unchaperoned—who have never once tried to make out with me and who consistently make me better, stronger, and more confident in my work and worth.

There might be places where women should not go alone, but the fight for equality is not one of them. My gratitude for the men who walk with us is enormous.

Mike Pence's policy is veiled in the guise of chivalry and respect, but it is a big part of the problem. It is a kind of misogyny, more subtle than that of his counterpart in the White House but just as toxic to women's health and well-being. Perhaps even more so, because it makes a woman's virginity and chastity—or her fidelity to one man—the ultimate measure of her worth. With these religious overtones, men can get away with treating women as less than equal, and it comes off as having respect and good manners. Thanks but no thanks.

When men in high positions of power achieve ninja levels of misogyny on a daily basis—seemingly without consequence to their public profile—we need a new language of empowerment. This reign of nuanced sexism continues to keep women out of positions of power *and* puts us in competition with one another for a perceived scarcity of influence. In this environment, trusting women and cultivating friendships with other women is an act of resistance.

AGAINST OUR OWN INTERESTS

I'd heard the phrase *internalized misogyny* before, but I'd never really seen such a stunning literal witness to its effects. In October 2016, just a few weeks before election day, NBC released an old audio tape of Donald Trump and former television personality Billy Bush in which they displayed some really grotesque views of women. This was the sound bite that everyone thought was going to end his campaign; Trump said he could "grab 'em by the p***y" and "when you're a star, they let you do it. You can do anything."

Anything.

In the days that followed, Trump (or rather, his handlers) issued a half-hearted apology that was really just a defense. "Locker room talk," Trump muttered, with an eye roll.

Defending the indefensible has really been his MO all along, so it was not a surprising response. But it was surprising that women were among his most vocal defenders.

One news segment in the days following the release of that tape featured a group of women gathered around on couches in what appeared to be a comfortable living room, and they proceeded to brush off the remarks as "locker room talk." They adopted the "all men talk like that around other men" argument that had been making the rounds on conservative networks and then continued to talk about why they were still going to vote for him.

I was speechless. I was also livid. I wasn't angry just at Trump and the culture that produced him. I was angry at these women. They were traitors! How could they vote against their own interests this way? How could they let themselves get suckered into this narrative?

A little voice in my head answered my own question: *internalized misogyny.*

Internalized misogyny, or internalized sexism, is the pattern by which women come to accept and believe the broader cultural messages about the lesser worth of women. In this reality, women don't just believe in their own limitations; they actively participate in the systemic oppression of women and girls, for example, by excusing "locker room talk" and voting for men who will limit the voice of women in legislation. Or they go to churches where men preach that women can't preach. Or they defend a coworker who harasses another woman in the office, nodding along sadly, "Yes, he's right. She really shouldn't dress that way." You get the picture.

The truth is, women often embody the narrative of patriarchy. We do it in a lot of tragic ways: we vote against our own interests; we defer or demur when men around us say subtly sexist things; we judge each other unfairly; we place our own baggage and expectations on another's experience of womanhood. Overall, we continue to show up for and participate in the systems and structures that harm us.

For instance, more than half of the white women who voted in the presidential election cast their ballot for Trump, according to exit-poll data collected by the *New York Times.* Meanwhile, 94 percent of black women who voted and 68 percent of Latina or Hispanic female voters chose Hillary Clinton, but 53 percent of all white female voters picked Mr. Trump.[5] This shows, again, that many women—especially white women— were willing to put aside his appalling treatment of and speech

about women, thereby playing a role in upholding the patriarchal culture that he represents.

But for my part, I'm over getting angry at women who will
blindly support a blatantly misogynistic politician, church
leader, or even employer. I'm learning to see them differently.
I know now that even my own animosity toward those women
is a product of patriarchy—a system designed to turn disenfranchised groups on each other rather than on the system that
keeps them marginalized. When women blame other women
for the way things are, we divert energy and focus from the real
culprits and enablers of the system: those who most benefit
from the disenfranchisement of half the population and have
everything to lose when women truly mobilize and unify their
voices for good.

Other women are not the problem—not women who voted
for Trump, not women who support churches that don't allow
women pastors, not even women who blame other women
for the evils of assault and abuse. Those women are not the
problem, but their behaviors and choices are symptoms of the
problem. Once we acknowledge that, maybe we can change
how we engage each other—and, by so doing, change how we
approach the destructive patterns of patriarchy.

If women could all get together on this, there would be no
stopping us.

HOW WOMEN'S POWER GETS CUT IN HALF

Later, two women who were prostitutes came to the king
and stood before him. The one woman said, "Please, my
lord, this woman and I live in the same house; and I gave
birth while she was in the house. Then on the third day
after I gave birth, this woman also gave birth. We were
together; there was no one else with us in the house, only
the two of us were in the house. Then this woman's son
died in the night, because she lay on him. She got up in
the middle of the night and took my son from beside me

while your servant slept. She laid him at her breast, and laid her dead son at my breast. When I rose in the morning to nurse my son, I saw that he was dead; but when I looked at him closely in the morning, clearly it was not the son I had borne." But the other woman said, "No, the living son is mine, and the dead son is yours." The first said, "No, the dead son is yours, and the living son is mine." So they argued before the king.

Then the king said, "The one says, 'This is my son that is alive, and your son is dead'; while the other says, 'Not so! Your son is dead, and my son is the living one.'" So the king said, "Bring me a sword," and they brought a sword before the king. The king said, "Divide the living boy in two; then give half to the one, and half to the other." But the woman whose son was alive said to the king—because compassion for her son burned within her—"Please, my lord, give her the living boy; certainly do not kill him!" The other said, "It shall be neither mine nor yours; divide it." Then the king responded: "Give the first woman the living boy; do not kill him. She is his mother." All Israel heard of the judgment that the king had rendered; and they stood in awe of the king, because they perceived that the wisdom of God was in him, to execute justice. (1 Kings 3:16–28)

When I think about how women turn their grievances on each other—instead of the true root of the problem—I think of those two women in 1 Kings who are arguing over a baby, each claiming that the child in question belongs to her. The story is likely a folktale designed to reinforce the wisdom and authority of the king, which is not surprising. What is surprising is how clearly such an old story can provide a clear metaphor for the ways the patriarchy can turn women against each other.

Clearly, one of these women is lying. I suppose there is the possibility that the woman whose baby died is suffering a delusion, following her traumatic loss, and that she truly believes the child is hers, but I doubt King Solomon—or the authors of this passage, for that matter—would have been aware of that psychological possibility. In any case, this story reinforces that troubling notion that *women can't be trusted,* and it places the women in hostile opposition to each other.

Also, the women are prostitutes. So we can add a healthy dose of slut-shaming into the mix here.

How does Solomon solve the matter? Well, not having a drug store genetic test at his fingertips (really, a quick trip to Walgreen's would have solved everything), he does what *any* good leader would do—he offers to *cut the baby in half* and split the difference!

It is a terrible story. Truly, how we managed to canonize this and attribute it to the wisdom of a great ruler is beyond me. It is not exactly the stuff of Sunday school felt board story—although I do recall seeing an animated version of this story as a child. Equally horrifying.

In any case. this appalling story does serve a function, if we let it teach us about the ways in which women's voice and worth becomes diminished when placed in opposition to other women. The man—with all the voice, power, and authority in this scenario—is literally holding a sword to the throat of a child, while the women are focused on tearing each other down. Say all you want that Solomon would not actually have killed the child—who knows, babies were pretty disposable back then (as were women). It's an image that sticks with me. Very often our laws, our culture, our economy, and even our religious organizations are destroying the lives of women and children. But rather than addressing the unjust system, we turn on other women, who are, perhaps, only a product of the same unjust system.

Again, cultivating deep friendships with other women—and empathy for women who may never be our BFFs—is an act of resistance against "divide and conquer" misogyny. The church can support the building of these bonds in some direct and indirect ways.

First, providing a space for women's ministry is important. I love church ladies. I mean, who *doesn't* love church ladies? They get shit done, and always have. Church women's groups can form some deep bonds within the life of the church. But I wonder if these internal structures can also perpetuate a sense of otherness that Christian women sometimes feel toward women outside of their particular brand of faith.

Too often, churches get into the business of "pink ghetto" ministries—a tongue-in-cheek term for ministries that gather and connect women while keeping them outside the more meaningful and transformative work of the church. These ministries, highly gendered and geared to uphold a certain ideal of "biblical womanhood" (an expectation that modern women should mirror the expected behaviors and norms of women in Scripture) often serve double duty. Not only do they keep women sequestered away from more visible, vocal forms of ministry; they also perpetuate the forms of internalized misogyny that make women complicit in their own subversion. Some Christian publishers have even added pink sparkly Bibles to the mix—because even Jesus loves a pretty princess party, I guess? These "pink" ministries—with or without the literal pink packaging—are just one more expression of patriarchy at work in the church, a creative way of keeping women in certain boxes.

The good news is that long before the evolution of comforting but inwardly focused "interest" groups, Christian women have known how to organize for good. Women's missionary societies helped form the fabric of life as we know it; these groups have been caring for the poor while also elevating women's voices for centuries now. We know how to do this. Now's the time to take that combined spirit of camaraderie and compassion and use it for the good of women everywhere.

In addition to connecting women with each other and organizing for outwardly focused mission work, the contemporary church needs to also find creative ways of equipping and empowering women for leadership within congregational life. For instance, I wonder how many women were, like me, raised in a church that told them they could be ministers but will still not call a woman to the role of pastor/preacher when the chips are down. The mixed messages we send our girls and women are overwhelming sometimes. Of course there is ongoing tension among women; when even the church has convinced us there is only so much room for us to speak and lead, it creates a sense of having to jockey for position.

But what if the church could learn to rise above its cultural influences and instead be transformers of the wider culture? To elevate a woman's voice in the pulpit is to empower women's voices in the wider community, and the church is uniquely positioned—more than any other institution or organization—to embrace that potential in our lifetime. What if we could create more room for women to lead, rather than enabling a sense of scarcity around that potential?

In theory, this sounds simple. In practice, it might take on different expressions in different contexts. For a church that does not have women pastors on staff, inviting women as guest speakers and preachers would go a long way. For any church, giving girls an opportunity to speak on youth Sunday (or any Sunday!) helps create that sense of identity and belonging that will give them a voice for leadership. Maybe we need to take our youth on field trips to hear women faith leaders from other traditions and to celebrate the ways women are empowered to lead within the Jewish or Muslim traditions or within other circles in our local community.

The possibilities for transformation are endless. When women are fully embraced and included in the life of the gospel—and reconciled to each other in the process—then the patriarchy doesn't stand a chance.

Questions for Reflection and Discussion

1. When have you seen or experienced competition between women benefiting the men already in power? How can women work together to counter the culture of competition and judgment that we've been influenced by?
2. Can you think of some examples of internalized misogyny that you've witnessed or experienced in your own life?

How can we break the influence of such self-defeating tendencies?

3. What is the problematic nature of "biblical womanhood"? How can church women's groups empower rather than limit women?

3
The Privilege Problem

Marian Anderson was an accomplished and well-known singer in the 1930s. When as a child she was denied entrance to music school ("We don't take coloreds," they said), her home church passed the basket, literally, to pay for private lessons. Later in life, she studied in Europe, traveled, and performed abroad. Yet, closer to home, she was not permitted to perform at Constitution Hall in Washington, DC. The Daughters of the American Revolution owned the building, and though they referenced some vague "rules and regulations" when they denied her use of their hall, the problem was clearly Anderson's skin color.

The good news is that Eleanor Roosevelt, wife of the U.S. president, resigned from the DAR over this episode, and ultimately Anderson gave a concert in front of the Lincoln Memorial on Easter Sunday of 1939.[1] That performance was attended by upwards of 75,000 people, with millions more listening over the radio. Even in a time that we would consider the dark ages in terms of both gender and racial equality, she was widely recognized for her talent and regarded as an extraordinary performer.

The bad news is that Eleanor Roosevelt couldn't fix everything. White America has been at work silencing the voices
of women of color, long before Anderson's time and, sadly,
long since. This is not true only of women performing in
high-profile places; it is a systemic injustice that reaches every
sphere of public and private life. We cannot blame that mar-
ginalization strictly on the patriarchy. White women have
been and continue to be perpetrators of this divide. It's time
that we, as white women (and men) in the age of daily microaggressions against minority women, fess up, learn more, and
move forward.

Many of the limitations within traditional feminism are
self-inflicted wounds. The conversation has too often been
limited to the ranks of educated, middle-to-upper-class, white
women. In the grand scheme of things, that makes for a pretty
small dinner party. It's no wonder we aren't further along on
the journey for full equality. How can women attain full equality with men when some women don't even entirely recognize
the full equality of all women?

Scholar, historian, and author bell hooks explores the experience of black womanhood in America—rooted in slavery, with
ripple effects all the way up until now—in her groundbreak-
ing, must-read book *Ain't I a Woman*. hooks titled the book
as a nod to Sojourner Truth's iconic speech, during which she
repeatedly shouted, "Ain't I a woman?!"

For much of European/Western history, the church's teachings about Eve's role in original sin—namely, that she lured
and tempted Adam to eat the fruit of the tree, thus leading to
the downfall of all humankind—led to a common image of
women as temptresses and the ultimate cause of (her) man's
downfall. But during the Victorian era, there was a gradual
shift away from this worldview for a while—when the "ide-
alized woman" came into play. In this image, women were
coddled, shielded from the world, and ultimately placed on
a pedestal. On the surface, this may have looked like honor;
but on the contrary, it was a carefully designed social construct

meant to keep women silent, subservient, and far away from the workings of the man's world.

According to bell hooks's extensive study and commentary, this shift had repercussions for slave women in the early to mid 1800s:

> The shift away from the image of white woman as sinful and sexual to that of white woman as virtuous lady occurred at the same time as mass sexual exploitation of enslaved black women—just as the rigid sexual morality of Victorian England created a society in which the extolling of woman as mother and helpmeet occurred at the same time as the formation of a mass underworld of prostitution. As American white men idealized white womanhood, they sexually assaulted and brutalized black women. Racism was by no means the sole cause of many cruel and sadistic acts of violence perpetrated by white men against enslaved black women. The deep hatred of woman that had been embedded in the white colonizer's psyche by patriarchal ideology and anti-woman religious teachings both motivated and sanctioned white male brutality against black women.[2]

Furthermore, white women's role in these instances—when they were aware, and when they acknowledged that white men were brutalizing female slaves—was not to be outraged at the man but to direct their anger *at the female slave*, as though an enslaved person with no agency was somehow complicit in their husband's/father's/brother's moral downfall. This might lead to further abuse by way of a beating or some other physical harm—whether enacted by the white woman herself or directed by her but carried out by another slave. Often it just meant the white female slave owner remained silent—and thus complicit—in the ongoing rape and brutalization of female slaves. Among white women who were involved in the movement to end slavery, sometimes what motivated them was not a benevolent desire for the slave's freedom but a desire to remove this "temptation" from the men.[3]

Of course, white men continued to sexually assault black women long after slavery was over. This painful truth is just one expression of the continued devaluation of black women's lives in American culture, a reality that continued to play out into the next century. hooks frequently points out the tendencies of revisionist history to change the narrative of our past, and once you start seeing the truth, she points out, you can't un-see it. For instance, in reading multiple books about the role of Christian women during the abolitionist movement, some sources highlight the antislavery roots of the women's movement. That is to say, that some of the very first organized women's groups in America were missionary groups focused on ending slavery. In that work of ending slavery, white women began to reflect on their own status in the larger society. This led eventually to a more organized effort for women's equality. As Barbara MacHaffie says,

> The abolitionists argued that all human beings had a right to life, liberty and the pursuit of happiness, and some women observed that they were a glaring omission. The abolitionists quoted Gal. 3:28 on behalf of the slaves, and some women began to realize that they, too, were included in the biblical promise of equality. The more some women thought about their own status, the more similarities they could see with that of the black slave.[4]

The profile and work of iconic women like Lucretia Mott, Elizabeth Cady Stanton, and Sarah and Angelina Grimké grew out of these same missionary roots. However, much mainstream history overlooks the ways in which white women often chose to elevate their own status at the expense of their black sisters, as that movement unfolded. hooks writes:

> The fact that the majority of white women reformers did not feel political solidarity with black people was made evident in the conflict over the vote. When it appeared that white men might grant black men the right to vote while leaving white women disenfranchised, white suffragists did not respond as a group by demanding that all women

and men deserved the right to vote. They simply expressed anger and outrage that white men were more committed to maintaining sexual hierarchies than racial hierarchies in the political arena. Ardent white women's rights advocates like Elizabeth Cady Stanton who had never before argued for women's rights on a racially imperialistic platform expressed outrage that inferior "niggers" should be granted the vote while "superior" white women remained disenfranchised.[5]

Yikes! That is a different story from what our history books—even church history books—tell us.

This is just one example of the ways in which even the most progressive white women have often sacrificed the interests of our sisters of color as we struggle for our own equality. It's also a great example of the ways in which we sanitize and "white wash" our history, our shared remembrance of how change happens. This adversely effects the ways in which we move forward in other times of transition. We can blame the patriarchy to a point—for disenfranchising *all* women and creating these dynamics. But at some point, in order for women to move forward toward a fuller kind of equity, white women need to own our historic and ongoing compliance in institutionalized racism in America.

As women began to take more of a place in the workforce, for instance, white women were given preferential treatment in hiring and were often paid more than women of color for the same positions. Ironically, one of the complaints that women (to this day) have about inequality with men is the ongoing pay gap! During the women's movement of the late 1960s, hooks points out, "[white women] urged black women to join 'their' movement . . . but in dialogues and writings, their attitudes toward black women were both racist and sexist. Their racism did not assume the form of overt expressions of hatred; it was far more subtle."[6]

It's those "more subtle" forms of racism that continue to plague efforts toward equality today. Alice Walker coined the term "womanist" to refer to the movement that emerged among women of color, to fill the void that Second Wave Feminism had left in filling their needs.

Still—after centuries of subjugation under slavery, then segregation, and then Jim Crow—there emerged in the African American community a mentality that it was now the time for the African American men to be given elevated status and power. As a result, African American women, as a group, assumed a role in the background of the new age of (relative) equality. They would endeavor to support black men, giving them space to assume the power they had been denied for so long.[7] The problem was that black men began to appropriate the same advantages that patriarchal rule had given white men for so long. So in many ways this was bad news for black women; with new rights and privileges elevated for black men, the women were still left on the sidelines.

Revisionist history comes up here as well. We tend to remember Rosa Parks as the matriarch of a revolution. She's iconized as a mild-mannered seamstress: matronly, mannerly, gracious. All that may be true, but that's not all she was. She was also an activist: fierce, intentional, and unafraid. She was not a woman who just up and decided one day that she was going to stage the resistance. She was part of an organized movement, chosen specifically for that role, in that time and place. She was one of the most active members of the NAACP in Montgomery, Alabama. Yet, when the black community of Montgomery held their next big gathering, at which she had expected (and was prepared) to speak, she was told by male organizers, "You've done enough."[8] She was not given the microphone.

So the world turns . . . for women everywhere, and especially for women of color.

SINS OF OUR MOTHERS

Such gross gender and racial inequalities are not just a thing of the past. The voices of women of color, like the voices of Marian

Anderson and Rosa Parks, are often co-opted even today—and not just by men, but specifically by white women. The Pantsuit Nation was a Facebook group that emerged in the run-up to the 2016 election. As the name implies, it was a community of feminists voicing support for the first-ever woman (major party) candidate for president (one who happened to be known for her pantsuits). It became a space for women to share the experiences of being a woman in America—which can be, let's just say, troubling, even in the best of times.

It was a place of solidarity, and after the election it became a space of shared grief for what almost was, but wasn't, and for how clearly the world still preferred a loud white man over an experienced woman.

As the online "Pantsuit" community—PSN for short—gained traction and evolved into a space for women to share their stories, it also became a space that demonstrated the painful truths about white privilege. The voices of women of color were never elevated or valued in that sphere. In fact, many shared that their experiences were swiftly shut down in that space, or their stories were never cleared for public sharing in the first place. Shortly after the election, the curator of the page struck a book deal—which seemed dubious, given that she was primarily sharing other women's stories—and the "nation" kind of crumbled. The book's cover (prerelease) sports images of women of varied age and race; but women of color say they are not represented in those pages.

The Women's March on Washington the day following the 2017 presidential inauguration galvanized hundreds of thousands of women nationwide and even garnered support and sister marches all over the world. The Web was full of amazing, powerful pictures of women—women individually, women in groups, women from all over—wearing sassy shirts and crazy hats and holding all manner of clever signs. One such sign, a picture of which was shared widely on social media, captured the essence of what happened with the "nation," and in many ways what has been happening with the women of this country for centuries. It said, "Where were all you nice white ladies when we marched for Black Lives Matter?"

It's a fair point. March organizers had received widespread criticism for seeming to exclude the voices and experiences of women of color in the planning phases. They worked to incorporate a more diverse worldview in the overall message, but while many considered the March an ultimate intersectional success, that one sign captures the tension between white women's privilege and the ongoing struggle of women of color to find a place in what many view as "our" movement.

We're more than a century past First-Wave Feminism and more than half a century past the civil rights movement. And yet, there are so many ways that the discourse around equality is still limited. The next wave needs to include the voices of women of color. In preparing to write this book, I had these lovely visions of gatherings around a table—or at the very least, casual field research, conversations in which I asked my friends and neighbors of color about what it's like to be a woman in this time and place, how we can be better allies, and how white Christians can better engage this work of reconciliation with our brothers and sisters of color. I still think those kinds of conversations are important, but I also know it is not their job to educate me. As someone who grew up in a fairly rural and predominantly white community—and by predominantly white, I mean there were maybe five black kids in my whole high school—it is *my responsibility to broaden my own horizons* and also to resist the white savior complex that plagues so much of Western Christendom. It is my job—as a white woman, as a person of faith, and as a person of good conscience—to learn my history, to nurture empathy, and to find productive ways to engage in this work, in my community and world.

People with privilege must learn to amplify the voice of those who have less privilege. So men, let women talk more. Read books by women. Create spaces for women to take leadership, use your connections to elevate women with leadership potential, Maybe even step aside sometimes and create space for a woman in a space that is typically dominated by men.

White people, read books by black women. Listen to music by artists of color. Support local businesses owned and run by Latina women. Support minority women who are running for office—because we need their voices in leadership, not because we want to make tokens of them. Step aside sometimes; amplify the voices of women who don't get heard much. Make space in places and conversations that are typically dominated by white people.

When you propose this approach in the typical mainline Protestant church, most likely it will go over like a ton of bricks, because for most white American Christians, privilege is so ingrained we scarcely know it's there. You can't really give up what you don't know you have. Even among progressive Christians, I often find resistance to the very idea of white privilege. The mentality of "I worked for everything I have" is a pretty pervasive Americanism. But it mistakes economic privilege for racial privilege. While the two are certainly intertwined, white privilege must be understood as the foundation for all other kinds of privilege.

Before we can begin to unwind the devastating effects of racism in this country, we must first acknowledge that almost every part of our cultural narrative is built on assumptions of whiteness. Flesh-colored bandages and crayons, for instance, are based on the skin color of white people. A single black or brown baby doll may grace the shelf with dozens of white ones. The smallest things, like this, reveal the truth that having white skin automatically means advantages in life, from day one. That's why naming privilege is the first step. It has nothing to do with "white guilt," and everything to do with transforming our systems. From there, we learn new rules of engagement, new ways of walking alongside, lifting up, and hearing those who have gone unheard for a long time.

Sometimes that means hearing a message that is uncomfortable for us to hear, or a message that is not necessarily meant for us in the first place.

CHECKING OUR PRIVILEGE

When Beyoncé dropped a super-secret new album—in the middle of the night, on a Saturday, on HBO—it was poetic and raw. It was gorgeous and also a little ugly. It was a mind-melting paradox of empowered vulnerability . . . or vulnerable empowerment. It was a sound nobody had heard women make before, with a razor-sharp edge, with something ancient about it. *Lemonade*, both the music and the visual story it tells, is art and story and song. As a *Rolling Stone* feature noted, the album was "structured around symbolic chapter titles, and touches on themes including black identity, marital infidelity, sisterhood, Christian faith and a final 'Reconciliation.' Black women surround and support Beyoncé throughout."[9]

And it isn't for me.

By that I mean not that I don't like it, but that it isn't mine. It doesn't *belong* to me.

Lemonade—in all its paradox and beauty and poetic suffering—isn't mine. If you're a white woman, it's not for you either.

If you're a white heterosexual man, it's for sure not yours.

If you're a gay dude? Debatable. Gay men have some kind of fierce fandom going out there that has its own rules, and I'll abide. I'm not going to tell you if it is or not.

I just know for sure it doesn't belong to me.

For those of us who happen to be straight, white, Christian Americans, we have almost every kind of privilege there is to be had. We are not accustomed to hearing from the entertainment industry—or any industry, for that matter—that we are not the target demographic for which some big thing is intended. This is what privilege means: to rarely, if ever, hear the words "This is not meant for you" aimed in our direction.

In this case, it's an especially hard truth to acknowledge, because she is *so amazing*. When she is dancing like a goddess, and sticking it to the boys club in her I-don't-give-a-**** shoes, we want to believe that she is every feminist fantasy that we have ever choreographed while sitting through a long meeting or boring class. (No? Just me?) But here's the truth we must hear in this new album: hers is the anthem, not of the single ladies, not of the run-the-world girls . . . but of strong women of color. As a white woman, it's not my song to sing. While I might rock along in the car, I can't claim its truth as my own. Perhaps the calling of white women, instead, is to learn to just dance along in solidarity and lend our voices as backup when we are able.

Ijeoma Oluo wrote:

> *Lemonade* is about so much more than one relationship and its infidelity. *Lemonade* is about the love that black women have—the love that threatens to kill us, makes us crazy and makes us stronger than we should ever have to be.
>
> We are the women left behind. We are the women who have cared for other women's children while ours were taken away. We are the women who work two jobs when companies won't hire our men. We are the women caring for grandchildren as our sons are taken by the prison industrial complex. We are the women who march in the streets and are never marched for. We are the women expected to never air our grievances in public. We are the women expected to stay loyal to our men by staying silent through abuse and infidelity. We are the women who clean the blood off our men and boys from the streets. We are the women who gather their belongings from the police station.[10]

You can say that her risqué costumes are the antithesis to feminism; but you'd be missing a big piece of the story. You can say that staying with her husband after rumored domestic violence makes her weak; but you'd be missing part of the story. You can say that she's sold out to big labels and corporations, but you'd be missing a big part of the story.

You can say that an album like *Lemonade* is too angry, too dark, too crass and . . . well, "colorful" in its language and imagery. If that's how you feel, then there's good reason: because maybe it's not for you. It's not for me either. But I will still listen. I will listen with deep admiration—not just for the art, but for the spirit and story it embodies. I will marvel at its strength and its witness. But I will listen as you might watch a rare bird in the wild—not to be touched, held, or owned . . . just glimpsed through dense branches. A blur of color, off to settle in its true home.

WHOSE TABLE IS IT?

In the church world, we often talk about "making more room at the table." That works in some contexts—especially if we're talking about the communion table. But sometimes I wince at the implication that "we" are the ones with the power to invite—with the ownership of the table that entitles us to extend an invitation. I wonder if, rather than finding ways of making room at our table, we would do better to support and lift up what women in other circles are already doing. Then it's no longer about inviting them to our show but showing up for theirs. In this way, we could do a much better job of the work of intersectionality and change the ways we connect across boundaries of race, gender, and even faith background.

For my part, I've tried to start watching the news and engaging the world with an eye and ear for what it says to and about people of color. I try to hear the story of Sandra Bland, for example, as a black woman who is raising black daughters and having to talk to them about what it means to be a woman of color in a world where the realities of police brutality are denied as fiercely as the realities of racism.

I watch with a new eye for Kamala Harris now. I see her interrupted over, and over, and over by her male colleagues, and I wonder how familiar this territory must be to her. I think about what barriers she's had to overcome to get where she is, and I worry about what kinds of torment she will face when she runs for national office (please, baby Jesus).

I watch Leslie Jones get hammered on Twitter, basically just for existing. I watch the Obama girls get called names that I hope my own children never get called in their lives. A friend from college shares a horrific story on Facebook about being targeted and harassed by a white male driver on the road. I try to bear witness. To hold all of these stories not as objective episodes tangential to my story and my faith but as integral parts of my experience of the world and who I know God to be. That positioning changes my outlook dramatically, from bystander to partner.

It's intimidating. I will screw up. You will too. That's why doing this work as a community—preferably as a community of faith—is so important.

That's why it's also encouraging to know that even Jesus screwed it up sometimes. (I know. Commence pearl clutching.)

But it's true. In the story of the Canaanite woman,[11] Jesus was on the road with the disciples (weren't they always?) when this woman approached and asked Jesus for help. Her daughter was being tormented by a demon, she said. While she didn't precisely ask him for a healing, she asked that he show her mercy. And Jesus, in fairly un-Jesus-like fashion, walked away. She was, after all, a woman. An ethnic minority. An outsider. She added up to nothing.

She kept on, though, because mothers do not quit. Then Jesus stopped and said to her, "It isn't fair to give the children's food to the dogs."

Maybe he was tired. Maybe he'd had a long day on the road, or he was distracted, or he was thinking very deep Jesus-y thoughts. But any way you shake it, that "dog" remark was a fairly pointed racial slur, as a matter of fact. He knew what he was saying.

"Even the dogs deserve the crumbs from your table," she said pointedly. Something in that simple image—or maybe it was her well-placed snark?—turned him around. He saw for a minute. His eyes were opened to his privilege—the ways in which the world was ordered with him in mind, and the tables were turned in his direction. Not because he was the Son of God, but because he was a man! And a Jewish man, at that. He had everything. She had nothing.

So he showed her mercy, and the Jesus we see after that is a lot more like the Jesus we are more comfortable with seeing.

Some biblical scholars call this the moment when Jesus gets woke.[12] True story. Sometimes all it takes is one relationship, one conversation, one real encounter with a person from outside of your assumption zone, to completely turn the world around.

I'd venture that many people are deeply disturbed by the notion that Jesus could have his mind, his heart, his perspective changed. It implies that he was not perfect—that he had, in fact, a deeply human and fallible side; that he was a product of his time and place and culture, every bit as much as you are or I am. While that interpretation may throw a wrench in the whole "fully divine/without sin" Christology, it does something else too: it gives us hope. If even Jesus had so much to learn, then there may be a big learning curve for us too. There may be some grace along the road. There may be meaningful transformation to be found, for the church and for the world.

At the same time, the Canaanite woman herself brings a meaningful word: in her brief appearance, she models the dynamics of "calling in vs. calling out." Calling out is when your neighbor says something racist (or sexist, etc.) and you call them out on it—directly and with no regard for hurt feelings. You say, "Hey, that was racist, and not OK!" There's a time and place for calling out. In fact, nice white Christians need to get a little more schooled in the fine art of calling out.

But what the Canaanite woman does instead is a calling in. Calling in is more nuanced than calling out. It is constructive. It offers the offending person a way forward without having to put them on the defensive. It puts the onus on them to dig a little deeper, to think more critically about the statement they just made. "Hey, Jesus, even dogs get the bread crumbs . . ." She might also have said, "I wonder what your mother would think about that, Jesus . . ." You get the drift. A call-in can be life-giving—even transformative.

Civil rights icon Ruby Sales recently gave an interview on the *OnBeing* podcast. She recounts the importance of her faith as she grew up in "southern apartheid" (otherwise known as the segregated South). She talks about how the narrative of faith she learned in church gave her a sense of belonging and identity much more powerful than any competing message she might have received from her surroundings. That faith story, she says, was at the heart of the civil rights movement, and the powerful nonviolent resistance modeled by Martin Luther King Jr. and his contemporaries. She then goes on to note how much that sense of belonging and identity seems to be lacking in any modern-day expressions of white Christianity. It is that vacuum of spiritual identity that continues to produce white supremacists, especially in the political climate that emerged in the 2016 campaign and election.

For Sales, the solution is to engage in the spiritual practice of asking, "Where does it hurt?"[13] People of faith need to get to work crafting a faith narrative for our time and place that does not just demonize racists but also gets at the heart of root causes of ongoing systemic racism. A conversation that seeks to understand the full humanity, not just of people of color, but of those who continue to spread hate and violence toward people of color.

In recognition of our privilege, perhaps white Christians and predominantly white churches in our time might go about cultivating the spiritual practice of calling in. We can equip our people with the language of invitation and transformation, so that they can both *call out* injustice as they witness it in their community and *call in* those who might otherwise be resistant to recognize their own complicity in that system.

It is the responsibility of white people of faith to shift this narrative and draw more people to the table for the conversation—not because the table is ours, but because lending our voices to this work means that our brothers and sisters of color do not have to bear the weight of the work on their own. In calling in, we create an invitation, not only to the work of justice, but to a way of life that is rooted in fellowship and equality. If we mean what we say about all being one, equal in Christ, then we have to name our complicity in these systems that continue to harm women and people of color, especially women of color.

Maybe the Canaanite woman, with her calling in of Jesus, can serve as a model for conversation about race and privilege in our own congregations. While our dialogue about racism should certainly not be limited to race as it relates to feminism, it is an important part of any discourse about women's empowerment in our own time. And it opens the door to the deeper conversations about equality that we should be having across all sorts of boundary lines within the family of faith.

Questions for Reflection and Discussion

1. What's the difference between "calling in" and "calling out"? Can you think of some examples of times you have witnessed each? Next time you're tempted to call someone out, how could you call them in instead?
2. Why is addressing white supremacy important in the work of equality for women? What factors continue to divide white women and women of color?
3. What other groups have potentially been marginalized by women of privilege, seeking their own gain at the expense of others?

4

Using Our Words:
The Healing Properties
of Inclusive Language

In the beginning was the Word . . . many, many words, to
be precise. Words that we later canonized and called Scripture, widely attributed to the authorship of God. Throughout
the history of the Christian tradition, these words have often
been approached as historical, scientific text—proof of God's
existence, sovereignty, and ongoing presence in the human
narrative. As a result, the document—as meaningful, sacred,
and life-giving as it can be—has also been misused in countless
ways. People of faith have used dubious methods of interpretation to uphold all kinds of systemic human ills, from slavery to
capital punishment to homophobia.

The use of Scripture to defend and institutionalize misogyny
is perhaps the most deeply entrenched and thoroughly actual-
ized misreading of all. Generations of Christians have superimposed a masculine worldview on both ancient and Gospel
texts. While both Hebrew and early Christian cultures had
their own share of male dominance, our more contemporary
readings have stripped much of the power that even women
of those times enjoyed. That history of subversion is so deep,
so complex, and so intertwined with the church as we know it

that we cannot possibly hope to mine the misogynistic roots of our faith tradition in any productive way.

But let's give it a try.

Yes, it is complicated and multilayered. At the same time, it's right there in front of us, in the text itself and in our history; so perhaps we can break down the evidence of a patriarchy-laced narrative in a few simple frames.

1. *The erasure from ancient texts of a largely androgynous God.* In the beginning . . . God was actually not a dude. That flies in the face of every flannel board lesson from Sunday school, every Charlton Heston movie, even the Morgan Freeman God of *Bruce Almighty*—whom I kind of dig, actually. But originally the Creation story depicted a divine being with both male and female characteristics, a God who looked down and created male and female "in our image." That "our" is loaded with contextual significance and has been mined for centuries by biblical-critical historians and scholars. Who is this royal we implied in the creative work of humanity? There are many theories, all interesting and with their own points of validity. But many of them point back to the same possibility—an origin, an omnipotent creator that was without gender distinction.[1] Such a figure would both defy pronoun classification and demand a descriptor more reverent and meaningful than just "it."

The Israelites also, throughout the Hebrew Bible, use fairly gender-fluid language to describe God. This was partly because their desire to avoid sins of idolatry made them averse to the notion of naming God too much anyway. They tried to be vague, in order to keep themselves from inadvertently creating graven images.[2] Furthermore, their use of language and understanding of divinity were broad enough to include images of God as both father and mother, provider, source of life and, in particular, of fertility.

2. *The erasure of a feminine Spirit.* Ancient Jews understood the Spirit of God to be the revealing of God's voice. That Spirit was understood as a feminine expression of the Holy, as was Woman Wisdom, as she appears in Proverbs. Her role was

to guide and inspire the holy prophets and generally to offer guidance to the righteous leaders of Israel. The word for this presence is *Hokhma* in Hebrew, and *Sophia* in Greek. That feminine presence of divine guidance appears throughout the Hebrew Scriptures.[3] Over time, though, Woman Wisdom lost her standing as a feminine expression of the one God of Israel and became a more symbolic, literary figure.

Similarly, the Holy Spirit was once considered a female presence; in some of the earliest Christian traditions, she was even understood to be the mother of Jesus! This Holy Mother, or Holy Spirit, meant that the third person of the Trinity was actually female in the early church. While she was not exactly omitted from early literature, she did gradually slip from prominence and take on a masculine presence, just like the other parts of the Trinity.[4] Over time, what we were handed was a three-person God as basically three dudes.

3. *The influence of the established church.* Over time, as the early Christian church evolved in a culture even more patriarchal than that of the ancient Hebrews, all of the more diverse images of God were blotted out in favor of the deep-voiced, hairy-chested God of our childhood Sunday school lessons. To the detriment of women everywhere, they were given, as a consolation prize, the role of being the downfall of men for all time. More on that in a minute.

Perhaps the greater sin here is the human insistence on reading the Bible as a history book or a science book, instead of acknowledging it for what it is: a narrative text exploring multiple generations' understanding of and relationship with God, and a multigenre collection of stories, poems, legends, and family memoirs that help humans understand their relationship with the Holy and with each other. As Walter Brueggemann says, "scientific, descriptive reporting is alien to the text and to the world of the Bible."[5] Reading the Bible in search of "fact" about the person of God is an exercise in missing the point. No book can tell us who God is, or what her voice sounds like, or what parts God has. But generations of Christians have approached the text in this way. So, in a way that has been extremely harmful to women, they have overlooked the simple fact that the people of Israel, long ago, understood God to possess both masculine and feminine qualities; frequently referred to God as a mother; and would not have been at all offended if you said that God was androgynous, or even had an "intersex" identity.

Why does it matter? Because over time the gradual removal or phasing out of the feminine divine has diminished the once-common assumption that men and women were created equally in the image of God. The notion that men are first, and that women are secondary and derivative, lays a firm foundation for the subjugation of women. Even for ancient Hebrews, reverence for a feminine divine being did not necessarily shape what kinds of authority and autonomy women were granted in daily life.

So the concern isn't only about the words that we use for God, but also about the words that we use for *naming other people*. Broadly speaking, inclusive language is about using a lexicon of words that value all of human life equally. As Lisa W. Davison, PhD, of Phillips Theological Seminary always tells her students:

> As such a powerful tool, language can be used both to include and to exclude. Words can speak a word of hope or they can be used to destroy all hope. Speech can build up a person in love or it can tear down out of hate. Words can indeed hurt or heal. The Israelites understood the particular power inherent in the act of naming something or someone. When the human ('adam) is brought a new animal, the human names the animal and thus is claiming a position of power over the animal world. Outside of the egalitarian garden, the man names his wife "Eve," and this signals the beginnings of a patriarchal culture in which men will have power over women.
>
> Without voices and often unnamed, women and other "outsiders" are excluded from human realms of power but certainly not from God's love. Time and again, the stories of Israel proclaim a God who takes notice of the powerless

and chooses those whom society deems "unworthy" to do God's will.

This concern for the marginalized and silenced was revealed again in the life and teachings of Jesus of Nazareth. The gospel stories show Jesus going against the exclusive rules of society to be among those who most needed to hear that they too were loved by God. As those who seek to follow Jesus, Christians are commissioned to proclaim the Gospel of God's radically inclusive love for all people. Gospel words should not exclude anyone from knowing God's love and grace. Rather, amid a broken world, Christians must speak into being a new reality of God's reign where all are welcome.[6]

The power of language has been used throughout the history of human relationship to claim ownership, to give identity, to build up or to tear down, to dominate and control or to make free. So the words we use for our fellow human beings are just as important as our choice of words and images for the Holy.

While the word "humanity" or "humankind" has taken the place of "mankind" in many mainstream, secular expressions, the full personhood of women still struggles to find verbal expression in all areas of culture, especially in the church. Our modern communities have not quite been able to outrun some of the more archaic language trends that shaped our earlier tradition. In fundamentalist and evangelical circles, the idea of God as father is just as sacrosanct as Scripture itself. And even the most progressive mainline Protestant churches still struggle to fully embody inclusive language in practice, even if they have adopted it in theory.

Some of this is because, let's face it, we pick our battles. While the clergy may have learned in seminary to take a more inclusive approach to naming God (and humanity in general), old habits die hard. Most churches value the practice of engaging multiple voices in worship, inviting laypersons to pray, read Scripture, and preside at the table, and we're not going to police every word that is spoken in our sanctuaries. It is neither practical nor desirable. We can teach the need for more diverse expression until we're blue in the face, but at some point we have to meet folks where they are and honor the words they choose for their own faith.

That said, we can sure keep trying. In fact, it's important that we do. Our insistence on using masculine normative language in the context of worship has harmful consequences for women that reach far beyond the sanctuary walls.

MORE THAN POLITICALLY "CORRECT"

In the church and beyond, many dismiss this conversation as mere political correctness, failing to recognize the real limitations our word choices place on women in the faith community and beyond. Furthermore, out there in the world there is a whole new lexicon of words used to harm and diminish women. We use slang terms for female genitalia when we want to imply weakness, for instance—terms like that p-word that the U.S. president uses to brag about his right to grab, without invitation. Use that word as a symbol of aggression toward women, and it is "just locker room talk." Use it in reference to a man to imply that he's weak, and it's suddenly the worst insult imaginable, as though weakness is so inherent to femaleness that all you need to do is conjure up the image of our body parts and you can effectively make another man worthless. If you use that word as an insult to men, what does that say about how you value women?

Obviously, there are other abusive words that the world likes to call women in general. If we are too loud and successful, we are bitches. Too assertive or alluring? Sluts. We could go on. With all the harmful and even violent words out there used to cut women down to size, silence them, and keep them in their place, it's more important than ever that the church work to redeem the language of gender. That starts with language for the feminine divine.

In *Her Story: Women in Christian Tradition*, Barbara MacHaffie offers a clear and concise apologetic for employing more inclusive language in the space of congregational life:

Many members of the Christian community view inclusive language as a trivial concern. . . . But many women point out that language patterns have grown out of and reflect cultures in which men ruled over women and controlled in society. By continuing to use this language, the church reinforces and maintains this social arrangement. . . . Language used for God is a fundamental part of this concern. The patriarchal context in which the biblical material developed is reflected not only in masculine pronouns for God but also in overwhelmingly masculine metaphors such as king, father [etc.]. . . . In the consciousness of people constantly hearing androcentric (male-centered) language, however, the idea takes hold that this language more adequately defines the divine. Communities soon come to believe that since God is fatherlike or husbandlike, fathers and husbands must be godlike. The male becomes the norm, representing humanity as it should be. The female becomes that which is different or the "other." . . .

The use of words like "mankind" and masculine pronouns in liturgies and hymns sends a message that women are not important. Women are invisible in the language of the worshipping community. Upon hearing and repeating this language the idea that women have nothing to contribute is reinforced. Men continue to be suspicious of women in positions of power and authority. Women are also bombarded with the message that they are nonpersons in the churches.[7]

Anyone involved in the life of the church knows that understanding the issues in play here is one thing, and being able to implement an intentional, consistent, and cohesive lexicon of inclusive language is another entirely. But there are resources available to begin or continue this important work in the local congregation. Many denominations have their own guidelines and materials available. Perhaps the most comprehensive

resource is the *Inclusive Language Lectionary,* issued by the
National Council of Churches.

To be sure, the practice of eliminating solely male language
from our liturgy and public life entirely is perhaps not an
attainable goal. Nor do I mean to suggest that we should never
refer to God as "he" or "Father." But if we're going to use those
words at all, we need to find an artful way of balancing the use
of those words with expressions for the feminine divine.

GOOD NEWS FOR EVERYONE

We must take care with our language to honor the value and
opportunity and quality of life for women and girls everywhere.
But we should not look at this dialogue through such a limited
lens, as something that benefits and elevates only the females of
the species. On the contrary, broadening our horizons of how
we name and recognize what is holy is a life-giving enterprise
for men and boys, as well.

There is tremendous push-back to the idea of raising boys
to be feminists. Because the language of feminism, though it
certainly should not be a girls-only club, comes across as inherently female. For so many cultural, sociopolitical reasons that
speak to the issue of patriarchy itself, the idea of making boys
more like girls is profoundly abhorrent to many people. What's
abhorrent to most of us, however, is the idea that being more
like women is something offensive.

We should be raising our boys around an ethic of equality.
Even if we don't call it feminism, boys should be brought up
with an understanding of the inherent worth of their female
counterparts. Not just for the sake of women and girls, but for
the benefit of the boys themselves.

Journalist Claire Cain Miller recently wrote an article for the
New York Times called "How to Raise a Feminist Son." There
is no open-comments section by which to view the reactions
of the public at large. (And—let's face it—it's probably just
as well, given the pervasive presence of Internet trolls.) In this

piece, she makes an excellent argument for the importance of raising boys without the strict gender codes of previous generations, not to make them "more like girls," but to open up more opportunities *for the boys* themselves. She talks about the ways in which we have begun teaching girls that they should overcome gender stereotypes, go for whatever job they want, and break down barriers; but we have not quite done the same thing for our boys. Girls have more choices than ever when it comes to toys, sports, activities, academic fields, and career choices, while boys are still conditioned to stay within some pretty strict confines of what it means to be male. For instance, they are discouraged from playing with dolls—even though playing with dolls is a perfectly normal way for boys to develop a sense of nurture that they would need as fathers. They are nudged away from the kitchen, from cooking and domestic tasks, even from pretend domestic tasks. What follows, of course, is that as adults they view those arenas and tasks as "women's work."

Even more damaging, they receive the message that they must be "tough" at all costs; they are urged to stifle emotions and discouraged from interests and activities that are perceived as being "just for girls." Miller notes:

> If we want to create an equitable society, one in which everyone can thrive, we need to also give boys more choices. As Gloria Steinem says, "I'm glad we've begun to raise our daughters more like our sons, but it will never work until we raise our sons more like our daughters."
>
> That's because women's roles can't expand if men's don't, too. But it's not just about women. Men are falling behind in school and work because we are not raising boys to succeed in the new, pink economy. Skills like cooperation, empathy and diligence—often considered to be feminine—are increasingly valued in modern-day work and school, and jobs that require these skills are the fastest-growing.[8]

Is this revelation still a tough sell in many circles? Yes. As much sense as it makes—and as important as it seems to give boys a truly "equal" view of the world and their place in it—messing with these small gender-based boxes that we place our children in is a recipe for great conflict and protest. In partnership with neuroscientists, psychologists, economists, and others, Miller makes specific suggestions for expanding boys' horizons. For instance, boys need strong men *and* women as role models; they need to be allowed to show emotion when they are upset, and not to be told to "man up"; they need to be given chores and responsibilities and taught to care for themselves and others (as opposed to relying on Mom forever, or at least until he finds a wife . . . you're welcome, future daughter-in-law). There are several other practical suggestions, but two that stand out as critical are teaching consent (no means no) and encouraging friendships with girls.

I have found cross-gender friendships to be a critical factor in my own life, both personally and professionally, and also in my role as a parent. If boys aren't taught to embrace the full equality of women at a young age, they will always be limited in how well they relate to women; and those barriers will affect everything from their marriages to their professional lives.

The language of our liturgy can go a long way toward overcoming some of these barriers, especially for young children who are in worship nearly every Sunday, or even on a semiregular basis. The words they hear in direct reference to God—in a place where they are being taught that their relationship with God is of utmost importance—will affect how they engage their faith for the rest of their days. It will also shape how they view themselves and their relationships with members of the opposite sex. Boys who hear gender-neutral or even feminine language for God at an early age will grow up thinking there is nothing strange at all about this! They will be better and healthier for it, as will the church.

Even as writers like Miller are penning a utopian world in which boys and girls are raised to grow up together as friends and equals, in the very same world, others are writing panicked missives about "the feminization of the church."

They say that when the masculine language is taken out of the hymns and women are leading worship, men don't want to sing anymore. They are saying that the more women take on roles in church leadership, the less involved men tend to be. They say that when the seminaries have an abundance of female students, fewer men go into ministry; that allowing women to be pastors makes the job less appealing to men; that gender-equitable language makes faith less approachable to men. Many folks out there, including some progressive-ish mainline Christians, blame the decline of the church on political correctness. In essence, they're saying that creating space for women's voices discourages men's presence in those same circles.

That is garbage. Where do we get this stuff?

Whether we are talking about church or some secular arena, we keep coming back to this absurd notion that *elevating the status of women effectively emasculates men and subverts manhood.* This is entirely untrue. What it does is challenge carte blanche male privilege. Equality challenges the notion that men have a God-given right to be in these spaces and women don't. But the goal is never for women to take over and kick the men out of the room entirely. The idea that women, in asking for gender-neutral language, are somehow out to take over and overthrow the world as we know it is absurd. It's absurd in the same way that white supremacist propaganda is absurd when it asserts that equal rights for black people somehow mean the erasure or genocide of the white race.

These worldviews of extreme sexism and racism both insist on the superiority of the white male, and both are utterly divergent from the true gospel. In its totality, the Bible tells a story, not of domination, but of the shared stewardship of creation, the full humanity of all, and life shared around the table. The integrity of every part of the Christian narrative relies upon the reality of an *imago Dei*, a divine Creator in whom we live and move and have our being, who gave us our identity, fully embodied, at birth.

Questions for Reflection and Discussion

1. Take a look through a typical Sunday worship bulletin or hymnal (from your place of worship or someplace else). How many words and images do you find referencing a masculine God, or referring to all of humanity in exclusively male terms (mankind, brotherhood, etc.)?
2. Would people in your faith community be comfortable using feminine language for God, on occasion? If not, why do you think that is? What would it take to nudge on those boundaries?
3. List all the words and images you can think of that would invoke female or gender-neutral images for the Divine. What are some ways you could employ these in the life of your faith community, if you don't already?

5

The Motherhood Myth

There's a church just down the road from mine that can always be counted on to have something folksy and also kind of oblivious posted on its changeable letter sign out front. You know, cringe-worthy little puns, or stuff that borders on nationalism for the patriotic holidays, things that are meant to be inviting but are really indecipherable for nonmembers. They change the sign on a fairly regular basis, but there is one thing I can always count on to cycle back through. Every year around Mother's Day, they put Proverbs 31:10 up there in giant letters:

A capable wife who can find?
She is far more precious than jewels.

The whole passage, of course, is much more involved than that little quip. Proverbs 31, in totality, paints a flowery vision of ideal womanhood, rooted solely in the woman's service to her husband and children. It talks about how her husband is known about town, elevated by her support and virtue; how her family is so well fed because she rises while it's still dark out to prepare the meals for the day; and how well dressed the children are because she makes all their beautiful clothes by hand. Of course in her spare time she plants and tends the family vineyard, cares for the poor, and basically burns the candle at both ends. There's some more stuff, but you get the gist.

That's great and all, and there's nothing inherently problematic with any part of this list of chores. But it is still troubling on many levels when a modern-day church advertises this notion as the life that women should strive for. First of all, like so many passages about women, it is taken broadly out of context, if we are to think of it as God's calling and chore list for all women everywhere. The book of Proverbs is actually a gathering of collective wisdom—poetry and proverbial sayings drawn primarily from sources outside of the Hebrew tradition. But the book's final twenty-two verses are yet another example of a text that has been used to sanctify limitations on women since days of old, however it may or may not have been intended.

The popular interpretation of this passage overlooks not only the original context of the literature—a woman of royalty speaking to her son about what to look for (and what not to look for) in a wife—but also the subtext that elevates the woman *beyond* the traditional home and hearth role. She makes major financial decisions for her family, runs a clothing business, and has a discerning mind in all things. In many ways, this text serves to point to gifts of generosity, industry, and intelligence that a good woman might possess. Much of that gets overlooked, though, when this passage is employed in praise of modern-day womanhood—or even as a directive toward modern women. It has become the stuff of women's devotionals, retreats, and, yes, Mother's Day sermons.

Scholar and professor Wil Gafney notes, "Biblical Hebrew does not have separate words for "woman" and "wife." (All wives are women, but not all women are wives, meaning that *isshah* can always be translated "woman" but not always "wife," which must be inferred.) Proverbs 31 never uses the common word for husband (*ish*), but uses a more hierarchal term, master/lord (*ba'al*), perhaps owing to its royal context. Like the Hebrew culture, our contemporary faith communities have also come to use those words "mother" and "woman" interchangeably—at least in spirit. That lack of nuance, coupled with our out-of-context Scripture readings, often enables those "pink ghetto" ministries that focus women's gifts and talents around all things related to home and children while directing those same gifts away from other areas of life and ministry.

This somewhat limited vision of womanhood, when glorified by the contemporary Christian community, makes a lot of assumptions about women's lives. It assumes that all women *want* to be wives and mothers, that all women *can* be wives and mothers, and that women who do become wives and mothers should find their deepest truth and identity in this role—even in the parts of the job that are a total drag sometimes. That is a lot of pressure. In many ways, it seems the Victorian "cult of ideal womanhood" has never really left us. Women, for much of history, have just been *expected* to pursue marriage and motherhood.

But for women of means and privilege, that life looks a lot different than it does for women living in poverty. So it follows that more privileged persons tend to romanticize that life of domesticity and nurture. In the process, motherhood gets compounded and confounded with all the other expressions of women's lives. While our lives have evolved in so many other ways, the specter of this "precious jewel" of a wife has hung over our heads. So, even if we are single mothers or not mothers at all, even if we work outside the home, even if we blaze trails in other areas of public life, there's still some vague expectation that we are aspiring to a life of tending the home fires and arranging a perfectly Pinterest-y pantry and keeping our perfect children clothed in hand-sewn garments. Fair-trade cotton, of course.

As a wife and mother myself, I can witness to the many great joys of family life. I count my children as the greatest gifts of my life and my marriage as one of the most challenging and deeply meaningful relationships in my life. But my experience of home and family life is just that: *my* family life. My experience and the joy I find in my own children and marriage should not be considered prescriptive for all womankind. That would be absurd. Yet it's how our culture has operated for the span of remembered history.

The ways in which our culture, both sacred and secular, has come to glorify motherhood ultimately does women more harm than good. This pressure to procreate and nurture and maintain the perfect nest probably isn't helping the kids and menfolk much either. Let's be frank here. Parenting is not everyone's gift, and not all women are called to be mothers. Some women who deeply desire a spouse and children do not find their dreams fulfilled. Furthermore, not all women who are mothers have the desire or luxury to be the kind of full-time, stay-at-home parent that a certain set of modern-day Christians continue to glorify, using texts like this one from Proverbs as their justification.

Many elements of the traditional wife/mother role, though certainly valid and life-giving for many women, depend upon a certain element of economic privilege. Want to be a full-time, stay-at-home mom, prepare healthy, homemade meals every night, make your kids' lunches, and take everyone to all of their many expensive after-school activities? Even if you don't have a family vineyard to tend, like that Proverbs lady, you might want to do some modern-day homesteading . . . backyard garden, canning, freezing, summer in the backyard with dirt under your nails, and then fall for intense food prep and nesting in for winter. That life, nowadays, requires that a woman have a spouse whose full-time job produces enough income to sustain the family. That single-income household, however, is a dwindling model compared to generations past. As the cost of living escalates and working wages stay the same, fewer and fewer women—even those who want to—have the option to stay home and do the full-time homemaking gig. Meanwhile, these domestic tasks, like canning and clothes-making, which many middle-class families now treat as hobbies, were once matters of pure survival—just the day-to-day business of eating and being alive. Yet we somehow have conflated all that with an image of comfortable domestic bliss. Ask my grandmother how blissful her years of tobacco farming were!

I'm not going to lie; some of that homemaking life sounds lovely. Some of it *is* lovely, and I'm grateful every day that I can pack my kids' lunch with healthy food, and fold their clean-smelling laundry, and be there to walk them home from school. But let's acknowledge that this is a life path available to only a few women in the world, broadly speaking. You have to find yourself in a pretty comfortable and affluent kind of situation to afford this lifestyle these days. In the modern economy, 57 percent of women hold a job outside the home, and 41 percent of those women are primary wage earners. Whether that is out of necessity or choice or a combo of both is rather beside the point.

The economic reality is that wages have not risen to meet cost-of-living increases over the past few decades, and very few American families are still able to live comfortably on a single income. There are about twelve million single-parent households in the U.S. economy right now, and about 80 percent of those are single mothers. More of us women than ever before—whether we work outside the home or not—have some kind of side hustle to supplement the family budget.

We'll talk more in the next chapter about the economic injustices inherent in this economy—and the specific injustices it implies for women—but for now we just need to acknowledge the reality that the church, in many expressions, glorifies a lifestyle and model of womanhood that much of the world cannot afford to enjoy. As Sarah Bessey said so well in her lovely epistle *Jesus Feminist*, "One of my friends has a saying: 'If it's not true in Darfur, it's not true here.'" He means that if we can't preach it in every context, for every person, it's not really for everyone, and so then we should probably ask whether or not what we are preaching is actually the gospel."[1] In other words, if a woman living in the inner city or the developing world can't fit her life into your box, then the box you're preaching is probably not God's vision for anything.

Women today are more empowered than ever before to live
without a man, to choose not to have children, to be economi-
cally secure and find meaning in friends, work, and creative
pursuits. Yet the societal and cultural pressure to procreate and
identify as "mother" remains overwhelming. In addition to the
limitations this pressure places on women who may not feel
called to the traditional wife and mother role, it sends harmful
messages to many other women: those who have not found a
partner; lesbian and trans women, for whom the role of motherhood might be fraught and complicated; and of course, women
who may truly want to be mothers but struggle with infertility.
For all of these and so many others, the church falls short if
we can't find ways of acknowledging and affirming a woman's
inherent worth outside of the parental and procreative frame.

How can we extract our ideas of womanhood from these
biblical and cultural confines while also fully embracing the
beauty of marriage and motherhood for those who find meaning in that path?

DITCHING THE PINK CARNATIONS

Most Sunday mornings, I take a few prayerful moments before
worship. I stand at the window, and I watch people come. They
come with hope and thanksgiving. They come with expectation and with heavy baggage. They come with joy, and they
come bearing gifts. Often they come with heartbreak. While
I don't always know what that is for each person, I often do. I
spot the one with the recent diagnosis; the one newly or nearly
divorced; the one struggling to make ends meet; the care-worn
one who just moved in with an aging parent; the one who is
doubting the very existence of God but still shows up to be the
church and to be with their people. I watch them approach,
and I pray for them. I pray for the wisdom of my words. I take
all this in, and sometimes, by the time I get to the sanctuary,
my heart is so full I can hardly breathe.

On Mother's Day, my parking-lot watch will show me happy, brightly dressed families with brunch plans after church. I am joyful with these families. I am grateful for these families. But I also see the woman who had a miscarriage . . . the man whose mother just died . . . the one whose mother was abusive or absent . . . the couple who has spent tens of thousands of dollars at the fertility clinic, without hopeful results . . . the ones who wait, and wait, and wait for the gift of adoption. Coming up the sidewalk there, I spot the woman who is expecting and hasn't told anybody yet . . . and the young couple who wonder if it is all worthwhile, or if the strain of parenthood might tear them apart. I see the mother whose child is breaking her heart today . . . and the man whose mother needs round-the-clock care and doesn't always remember his name.

I also see the ones who have chosen other life-giving paths over parenthood but feel ever-so-slightly judged when it is time to celebrate mothers.

I remember from childhood those days of someone pinning a pink carnation on all the moms and having them stand in worship for a round of applause. I know many churches still do something like this. The Baptists down the street will put an out-of-context verse about women on their changeable letter sign. The lectionary blogs share special litanies of motherhood. But I suspect that the joy these practices bring to a few is far outweighed by the pain they bring to many.

I also wonder if the whole Mother's Day thing has run its course—at least in the context of worship life—for the same reasons another event I remember from my childhood church days is problematic. Once a year we had Women's Sunday. Not related to Mother's Day, this was a day when women served communion, preached, led music, and said the prayers (otherwise known as Every Sunday in some of our places, these days). Days designated specifically to celebrate and venerate women are complicated—not just for the motherless child or the childless woman—because of their deep-seated, societal implications about what being a woman *means*, what women should look like, how they should act and dress, what roles are appropriate for them. The Ladies Lead Worship thing (even though my home church had women deacons and, for a while, a female associate pastor) subtly said that women leading worship is a special occasion—and aren't we all good sports for hearing what they have to say today?

Much of the cultural stuff around Mother's Day feels similarly condescending. The department stores are full of brightly colored, floral sheath dresses and big banners that say, "Mother's Day is May 10!" Meanwhile, television commercials show men with perfect teeth giving flowers to tearful women. Jewelry stores remind me of all the virtues of womanhood in their own way. I don't know precisely what those virtues are, but they probably involve a hot glue gun, which I should have bedazzled and galvanized as a charm for my new Pandora bracelet (which will coordinate with my pink dress). Is this because I need to look like an Easter egg to receive my breakfast in bed and pink carnation? No, it's more that I should want to look pretty and feminine to receive the honor that I have coming to me.

Call me crazy. Say I'm overly sensitive to cultural norms that are mostly harmless; I'm ruining a perfectly lovely day by wanting political correctness; or I'm just angry that I'm not a man. That's what such a cultural critique usually gets me in response. But I'm more concerned with validating those who share in my questioning: those who, like me, struggle with the feeling that something about this day reeks of placating the little woman so she won't mind the other 364 days when she does the drudge work/keeps her silence/doesn't get the raise/ loses the election.

Questions around ideal womanhood remain closely related to how we approach motherhood in church. If we aren't careful, we can easily fall into what Hallmark—or Macy's or the fundamentalists down the street—say a woman should be (and what she should look like) and miss the gospel wholeness inherent in all God's people.

All that said, we should all celebrate our own mamas however we choose. Every family should feel free to show their love and gratitude in a way that is authentic to them.

Meanwhile, the church needs to tread lightly, not just on Mom-centric holidays but on every ordinary day, and to think critically about the messages we send to women and about women. Are we honoring all kinds of women, not just the ones that stepped out of a mid-century sitcom? The CEO and the single mom working two jobs; the happily married, the intentionally single, and the recently divorced. The couple whose marriage is recognized by the state, and the ones who still fight to have their union fully recognized by all. The "virtuous," and those trying really hard not to scream obscenities at their unruly children. The one who rocks that new Lilly Pulitzer dress as if it's her job, and the one who would not be caught dead in pastel. And the ones—all the ones—who taught us about Jesus, using only popsicle sticks and a felt board. Those women are love incarnate, and they are mothers to us all.

All of these women are children of God and have made valid life choices based on circumstance or their own unique experience and worldview. Whatever happens in worship has to be for all of them. Because we are all the body of Christ, together, and nobody gets to tell us what that looks like.

Do we who are called to be Christ's body in the world know how to meet all of these women where they are? Does our language in worship acknowledge these many and complex realities? Are the programs that we offer at church inviting to women at many different ages and life stages? Or are they specifically designed for the twenty-something to forty-something married mom with 2.5 kids at home?

There's no one right answer here, nor is there an easy answer to unwinding years of socializing women into tiny boxes. But a theological and practical awareness of these complexities can help our local congregations develop more meaningful and authentic relationships with all kinds of women, employing the gifts of many for the work of the gospel in the world.

PUTTING PARENTHOOD IN PERSPECTIVE

The modern-day church as we know it thrived for generations on this glorified model of home and family life. Through a careful combination of prescriptive narrative, guilt, and family-based programming, the church perpetuated the family model that fueled its growth. But now that fewer and fewer families fit into the traditional box—two heterosexual parents, 2.5 kids + dog/cat/goldfish situation—the church struggles to maintain its relevance. Of course, there are many more cultural, economic, and spiritual factors at play in the decline of the modern-day church. But at the heart, the church's unwillingness to adapt to the changing trends of family dynamics has made many people, and many groups of people, feel there is no place for them in the life of the faith community.

The call to redefine and re-envision faithful womanhood then serves multiple purposes. Not only does that reframing work to empower women and speak to that inherent ethic of human worth; it may also strengthen the church for coming generations, if we can find ways to be inclusive of different expressions of family and femininity.

So how do we honor the gifts of motherhood without placing a woman's sole identity within the confines of that one role? We can start by learning and acknowledging the socio-economic factors that affect women's lives and choices. Health care, child care, education, opportunity, income, and other practical factors play into a woman's decision to become, or not to become, a parent and when. Our job should be not to judge those decisions but to work for equality, not just in theological and philosophical ways, but in practical ways. Having access to things like affordable health care, affordable child care, and equal pay will make life easier, more just, and more equitable, so that women can chart the life course they desire.

Add to this matrix of factors the current situation of young adult women. That coveted Millennial faction that the church already struggles to engage (to the point of obsession, some might say) has increasingly put parenthood on the back burner. Of course, this is not true across the board, but broadly speaking, compared to the patterns of the generations preceding them, the birthrates are definitely trending down. Some of this can be attributed to the advancement of women over the last few decades. With more opportunities available to them, women feel more empowered to postpone or even forgo having children and to build a nonetheless meaningful life and network of relationships.

Some of their considerations are distinctly economic. With the rising cost of tuition and the stagnant state of wages (especially in low-paying jobs typically held by students) this generation has more college debt than any other. Compound that with the recession that hammered the country when this group was entering young adulthood, and you have a perfect storm of . . . well, whatever is the opposite of a baby boom.

Sociologist Phil Cohen writes,

> Most of the fertility effect on the recession was felt at young ages, as women postponed births. The oldest Millennial group was in their late twenties when the recession hit, and it appears their fertility was not dramatically affected. The 1985–89 group clearly took a big hit before rebounding. And the youngest group started their childbearing years under the burden of the economic crisis, and if that curve at 25 holds they will not recover.[2]

Not only is motherhood being delayed or decided against; furthermore, if you do have children, they will live with you in your home for maybe only a fourth of your life. Though women who have raised children will still always identify as mother, parenting becomes perhaps not the sole purpose of her days, once children have moved out. If we effectively condition women to believe not only that parenting is a deeply meaningful point of life, but that it is *the* point of their life, what does that do to their sense of purpose and worth when they naturally age out of that part of life?

Earlier waves of feminism struggled with mother as a defining role as well. In the early 1960s, as the boomer generation

was beginning to age out of the house and enter young adulthood, their mothers—the generation that had yielded the
boom itself—were left wondering what was next. Journalist
George Gallup wrote a profile of the typical American woman
for the *Saturday Evening Post*. In this piece, he noted, "One real
problem shows clear in the silhouette we have cut: the empty
years to be faced by the typical American woman—perhaps
half her lifetime—after the children are grown and gone. She
has not prepared for them."[3] A feature in *Newsweek* put it in
even starker terms. In a piece meant to shame the growing
numbers of dissatisfied housewives into recognizing that "biology was their destiny" (I know, gross!), a columnist stated that
"the average housewife has forty-five years of leftover life to
live" once her children leave home.[4]

"Leftover life?" I don't know about you, but I know plenty
of women who fill that time quite nicely. They aren't exactly
sobbing into their mimosas as they lounge by the pool, either.

The world in which women's lives were viewed in this way
is, I am thankful, foreign to me. That world is so foreign to
Millennials that many of them don't even consider themselves
feminists in the traditional sense of the word, because they see
the need of such characterization as long gone. But here again
we see the error of traditional feminism. It lacks the nuance
necessary to deal with newly evolved kinds of sexism. While
women's post-childrearing years may not be seen as "leftover"
and pointless these days, there are still subtle cues along the
way that say the decades with kids at home are "the best years
of your life!" Or how about the pressure to "*enjoy every minute*," forgetting that parenting is exhausting and tedious, even
for the happiest, proudest parents among us?

For some women, motherhood may not be the most fulfill-
ing part of life. And that's OK. At some point, we've bought
into the notion that other women's choices must, by default,
be viewed as a direct critique of our own. It benefits the male-
dominated status quo for women to see each other as threats.
Essentially, it keeps us from really ever getting our act together
and gaining full equality. As long as we can sequester ourselves

in little pods of "stay-at-home moms," "career moms," "intentionally childless," "single parenting like a boss," and so forth, we will always come upon a problematic "us vs. them" mentality. Our energies thus diverted, we become more invested in shaming other women than in working toward justice for women.

The good news is that the mommy wars seem to be winding down. Younger women (by which I mean younger than me) seem to be cultivating a "live and let live" mentality among their tribe; and women of every age are learning that we all fare better when we support each other's life choices and work together, for the good of our families and communities. Perhaps our notions of what it means to be a faithful woman can also evolve beyond the binary terms we've so long relied upon to define us.

MORE THAN A FAIRY TALE

If we truly want to explore women's lives and stories from a biblical perspective, we are going to have to dig a little deeper than Proverbs 31—which, in its original context, was a queen's letter to her baby boy. And probably a fictional queen at that! Knowing its limitations as a historical document, we're going to have to read Scripture for what isn't there—what's been omitted and subverted—as much as what is there. Enter Mary. The mother of all mothers.

Of course, this is complicated too. Mary, more than perhaps any other biblical woman, has been put on that pedestal of perfect mother, which removes her from real-life women and their struggles, on a platform that keeps her saintly and infallible . . . and in no way relatable to the hot mess of most of our actual lives.

But Alice Connor, an Episcopal priest and campus chaplain, has another take on Mary that, I hope, can blow the doors open on the whole myth of motherhood that aims to keep women relegated to traditional roles:

We call her the greatest mother who ever lived and also an unwed teen mom. We say she was perpetually a virgin and that she had several more kids after Jesus. Mary meek and mild. Mary accepting of what comes. We certainly don't think of her like fiery Ezekiel or lamenting Jeremiah. They had a word to speak to the people, and Mary is just, well, she's just a mom, isn't she? We moms do a lot of things and have a lot of responsibilities, but in the end, it's all about hearth and home. That's what they'd have you believe. I don't know who "they" are, but they're pretty convincing, aren't they? Somewhere in an unused storeroom in our brains, we know that's not right. It's not right that anyone is "just a mom," and it's not right that Mary was "just a mom" either. She's got something different going on, but it's something we've had a hard time putting our finger on. . . .

While Mary's first story is obviously a birth announcement, it much more closely fits a different form of biblical writing, the prophetic call. [Hers is a] prophetic song: the Magnificat. I'm not sure why we've lost the image of a prophetic Mary. We are left with a quiet, obedient mother without the firebrand language of the Magnificat, but that song is just as much a part of her as beatifically giving birth in a stable. Mary is more complex than we remember, more challenging than we expect.[5]

Surely we can recognize this as good news for all women everywhere. Mary was a powerful and prophetic preacher, an advocate for the poor and the marginalized, a voice for the weak, and, yes, she was also a mother—but never *just* a mother.

No women are ever *just* mothers. Women are never just *not* mothers either. We "contain multitudes," as Walt Whitman says, and are so much more than any one part of our being.

There are plenty of biblical women to provide models of strong and faithful living. Some had children, some did not. Some struggled painfully with infertility, while others had babies like rabbits and pretty much birthed the whole of humanity, not to mention all the tribes of Israel.

What a healing thing it would be if real-life, modern-day Christians could lift our archaic layers of restrictive cultural history from the pages of these rich and meaningful stories and see, beneath the dust and the grime, the more expansive and holistic story of God's vision for all people. In our multicultural, hyper-connected, quickly evolving world, a bigger picture of faithful women—not reducing the whole of female kind to a few verses of Scripture or some cameo of our grandmothers captured from a completely inaccurate snapshot that we can never quite hold anyway—could be life-giving for our own spiritual development and for the church we love. Theology is important. Scripture is important. An ethic of broad-reaching human worth is deeply important. But maybe the best and most life-giving thing we can do is remind each other that there is enough time to experience more than one expression of womanhood in a lifetime.

This is a conversation I find myself having frequently in ministry. A young mother (or father, for that matter) is feeling completely overwhelmed and saturated—with life, with work, with parenting. She is feeling guilty, because guilt seems to come with babies these days, straight from the delivery room, along with the funny hats and blue and pink striped blanket, and the plastic bracelet that you wish they could wear forever to let you know where they are. Guilt is standard issue. Parents are feeling guilty for working and leaving their babies in the care of others. Or they are feeling guilty that they've wasted their years of education and vocational training, abandoned their colleagues and their field of expertise, perhaps abandoned the whole world that is waiting for their next great breakthrough.

What I find most amazing is that sometimes parents can feel the weight of *both these things at once*. When they are at home, they feel guilty for not being at work; when they are working, they feel the weight of not being with their children. It is a truly vicious cycle, rooted in both the corporate lie of finding our worth in productivity and the supposedly biblical lie of perfect motherhood.

When I come into contact with a parent who is living with this struggle—in some ways an age-old struggle and in other ways a brand new horizon—I tell them this one thing: "There are seasons."

Which means—no prescriptive speech implied here—you don't have to be/do/hold everything right now. Not all at once. If you want to be home with your kids, that does not make you a professional failure. If you want to go conquer the corporate or scientific world, that does not make you a bad or absent parent. If you want to forgo the whole kid situation entirely? Good for you, we're getting a little crowded around here anyway. And if you change your mind later? That's fine. Through the wonders of science and adoption, there are options. Somewhere along the way, we've bought this notion that it is all or nothing, all the time. While life is fleeting and uncertain, and tomorrow is not guaranteed, chances are pretty good that you've got a few tomorrows stacked up in your favor. Trust your gut. Tune into your God-given gifts of discernment about what is right for *your* life, and *your* family, at this particular moment.

There are seasons. There is time.

Freedom to choose our life's path is the ultimate goal of the work of equality. This wide-open frontier of choices that lie out there for each of us, in this day and age, can leave us feeling overwhelmed; but if we truly have all the resources and support that we need, then women can see those horizons as a gift, and not such a great burden, if we find the space, and some grace, to let things come in their time.

Questions for Reflection and Discussion

1. What has been your experience of the "Proverbs 31 woman" archetype? What role has faith played in your discernment around marriage and parenthood?
2. What are some ways that your community of faith may be excluding women who are not mothers, for whatever

reason? How might your church or faith group be more inclusive of women who have chosen another path?

3. Are there ways to honor and celebrate motherhood without excluding, shaming, or judging women who have chosen another path?

4. What are some ways we might invite women who are mothers to be authentic about the struggles they face in balancing home, work, identity, and other values with motherhood?

6

Equal Pay and Representation: Why Is This Even Still a Thing?

Elizabeth Warren stood on the Senate floor to oppose the nomination of Jeff Sessions as attorney general. She spoke as part of her job as an elected official. She spoke as an American citizen. She spoke as someone concerned with the fair and equal treatment of all people, by the system that is entrusted with protecting the rights of all. Her statement was not adversarial or inappropriate in any way; in fact, she primarily used Sessions's own words to illustrate why she thought he was unfit for the job.

She was told to sit down and shut up. She was repeatedly told to stop talking. When she didn't comply, she was escorted from the room.

She spoke as a professional and as a leader. But in return she was addressed as a woman who was in the way, who had overstepped the bounds of her "place" and tried to influence the space she was in.

Regardless of your political leanings, in that room, at that moment, Warren was Every Woman. She was every woman who has ever made her way to a place of authority, only to be told, once she got there, that her voice didn't matter.

In defense of booting her from the room, Senate majority leader Mitch McConnell said, "She was warned. She was given a reason. *Nevertheless, she persisted.*" He said this as though a warning alone should be sufficient to silence any woman who challenged him; being given a reason was a bonus, a courtesy extended. If the warning didn't work, then the "reason" should have *definitely* shut her up. He then added her persistence as the final nail in the coffin, the transgression that justified anything he had to do to remove her voice from the room at that point.

#ShePersisted went quickly from trending hashtag to a lasting rallying cry for women on both sides of the aisle—and far beyond the political sphere, as well.

Not long after that, Senator Kamala Harris was questioning witnesses in a Senate committee hearing. The topic was an investigation of possible Russian interference in the 2016 U.S. presidential election. Again, this was a woman serving in an official capacity, to which she was elected. Again, she was speaking as part of her actual job. Again, she was silenced. They interrupted her. Repeatedly. They persisted, in fact, in interrupting her. It was right there on the television screen for everyone to see. This is a living diorama of American womanhood: say things out loud in a roomful of men, and they will make sure you do not have the last word. Again, regardless of party line, Senator Harris was Every Woman. We watched with both a maddening rage and a sigh of resignation and solidarity.

Not long after that incident, the *New York Times* ran an op-ed by Susan Chira about the universal nature of Harris's experience: "Academic studies and countless anecdotes make it clear that being interrupted, talked over, shut down or penalized for speaking out is nearly a universal experience for women when they are outnumbered by men."[1]

Throughout the history of the American women's movement, women have been treated first with disregard and then, when they persisted, with outright hostility. Once women won the right to vote, it was decades before they began to establish any real presence in the government itself. Essentially, they had earned the right to vote . . . for whichever men they wanted to be in charge.

That began to change in the early 1960s as the National Woman's Party began in earnest to push the Equal Rights Amendment through the U.S. Congress. At that time, there were two women in the Senate, and seventeen women in a House of Representatives of 435. Both of the senators and half of the congresswomen had inherited their seats from husbands who died while serving. (For decades, this was the only way a woman could serve in a national elected office.)[2] The Kennedy administration, responding to (well-justified) accusations that women didn't have enough presence in their White House, established the Commission on the Status of Women. The Commission was meant to be "modestly useful but not controversial."[3] That Commission, though meant to be a symbolic gesture and not a real policy move, succeeded in assembling a group of smart, accomplished women who began to talk in earnest about women's rights. Things began to move a little more quickly for women after that.

Ironically, one of the biggest leaps forward for women came from a man who was adamantly opposed to equality. Congressman Howard Smith of Virginia was serving as chairman of the House Rules Committee in 1964 when the Civil Rights Act was up for debate. Its most controversial section was Title VII, which was to prohibit racial discrimination in the workplace. Knowing that he did not have the votes to stop the act from passing, he did anything in his power to obstruct the process and delay the vote. As the guy in charge of the rules, he could do that (which is typically how the boys' club works, after all).

So what did he do, in order to gum up the works? He offered an amendment that would add *women* to the groups protected from job discrimination. He did this knowing full well the amendment would not pass, but hoping it would slow down the inevitable progress toward equal rights for people of color. To him—a man who was a representative of our entire government, in that moment—the equality of women was as ludicrous as the equality of black men. Let that sink in for a moment. It was not so very long ago.

The debate that ensued showed that Smith was by no means alone in thinking this was a ridiculous notion. Even to many of the leaders in favor of the Civil Rights Act, the notion of women as equals in the workplace was downright ludicrous. But Representative Martha Griffiths of Missouri was determined that women be included in this legislation. She once said,

> In my judgment, the men who had written the Equal Employment Opportunity Act had never even thought about women. [The authors] wanted to give black men some rights, and that black women would be treated like white women. I made up my mind that if such a bill were going to pass, it was going to carry a prohibition against discrimination on the basis of sex, and that both black and white women were going to take a modest step forward together.[4]

Thanks to her persistence—and that of other forward-thinking leaders—the measure eventually passed in the House, and later in the Senate. Years after it was signed into law, an aging Howard Smith ran into Griffiths in the Capitol. She said to him, "You know, our amendment is doing more than all the rest of the Civil Rights Act." His response? "Martha, I'll tell you the truth. I offered it as a joke."[5]

There, in a nutshell, you have the history of women's progress in America. Every step forward has been viewed as "a joke" initially—often even to those who were part of its progression! At every turn, women have persisted through the same pattern: first dismissal, then hostility when they didn't back down.

Once elected, women in power still have to fight for a voice in legislation. At this moment in our history, we have more women serving in the Senate and House than ever before. One hundred and five women serve in Congress right now, an unprecedented 19.6 percent of the total. Twenty-one U.S. senators are female at the moment. More women of color hold these positions now as well. Yet in President Trump's administration there are the fewest women in appointed positions since the presidency of Ronald Reagan.[6] Even the relatively high number of women in elected positions does not make for anything resembling equal representation.

Early in 2017, we saw an image that could be placed in Webster's dictionary next to the word "patriarchy": a roomful of white men—no women, no men of color even—surrounding a smug-looking president as he signed a bit of legislation that would affect the state of women's access to health care worldwide, a "gag rule" preventing providers from giving women complete and accurate information about their health. It was the first of many images that would emerge over the next months—images of men happily deciding the fate of women's bodies, not just at a national level, but globally.[7] As one such gathering (of men) debated whether or not maternity care and mammograms should be considered essential treatments covered by all health insurance policies, Senator Pat Roberts, from the state of Kansas, blithely quipped, "I wouldn't want to lose my mammograms!" Because boobs are silly, I guess? Because breast cancer is a joke? He later apologized. But he still supported removing the coverage requirement.

His comment reveals a truth of the effects of patriarchy on public policy making: when there aren't enough women physically present in the room, women's actual physical bodies can be regarded as unessential at best and problematic at worst. Women literally end up paying more for certain healthcare services and for coverage in general, because of the decisions made in these political dealings. When "no one else is in the room where it happens,"[8] subtle nuances make their way into our legal system that make having a female body a costly endeavor. Someone, somewhere, benefits from these penalty fees that we pay for having breasts, a uterus, and ovaries. Someone, somewhere, benefits from the liabilities of our physical frames, and it's not women who reap the rewards.

That's the problem with a relative lack of representation. It's not just about the optics of having women in the room.

That lack of voice literally affects women's lives, both at home and abroad.

SUPPORTING WOMEN, SUPPORTING FAMILIES

The political realm is not the only place where women's lack of representation creates systemic harm. When we look at corporate America and our entire capitalist system, we begin to uncover the troubling depths of what it literally *costs* to be a woman in the United States.

In her sweeping work *Taking on the Big Boys,* Ellen Bravo explores the many ways that a lingering wage gap and a shortage of leadership opportunities for women perpetuate a major social problem, namely, systemic poverty. She argues that "the heart of the pay gap lies in how society values what women do."[9] More than that, she shows the ways in which the people who work the hardest to perpetuate patriarchal systems are the people who benefit from those systems—not just in symbolic power but in tangible, fiscal terms. It isn't just women who suffer the consequences of these systems; it is families. In the same way, families on the whole benefit when inequalities are removed.

One of the most glaring truths revealed in Bravo's book—which, by the way, should be required reading for anyone participating in our modern-day economy—is how little the workplace itself has changed since women entered the workforce decades ago. Most of corporate America still operates on the myth that every family has a parent staying at home full-time.[10] In reality, a stay-at-home parent is a diminishing trend and a luxury of the upper middle class in most cases. Yet, even with only about 14 percent of American households enjoying the benefit of a full-time adult at home, our maternity and family-leave policies are archaic compared to those of the rest of the developed world. Childcare costs are skyrocketing. Women's earning potential is still, on the whole, nowhere near that of men.

Women now make up more than 47 percent of the American workforce, according to the Women's Bureau of the Department of Labor.[11] That may sound like a big step toward equality, but digging a little deeper, we find that 12 percent of women live below the poverty line, as opposed to about 7 percent of men. More broadly speaking, on average a woman still earns 73 to 77 percent of what a man earns in his lifetime, and the current wage gap checks in with women earning about 80 cents to the men's dollar.[12]

All this adds up to a sobering bottom line: women are simply working longer and harder, but for less money. Think about the socioeconomic impacts of that truth for lower-income American families. The uphill battle to make ends meet is becoming insurmountable, as healthcare and childcare costs increase at unchecked paces. Additionally, a growing number of women are now the primary or sole wage earner of the household, which compounds the situation. Women are responsible for more while earning less. The average household's income is *decreasing*, even as the cost of living rises dramatically and women work more demanding hours to keep up.

About 13 million American families right now are single-parent households; of those single parents, 80 percent are single mothers. Many of those single mothers are in low-wage jobs, with not a lot of hope for upward mobility, because the corporate structure is not designed to accommodate working women with children. At the same time, many of those primary-wage-earning women are making less than their male counterparts in similar jobs.

The implications for our overall economy are depressing.

As long as imbalances exist at the top of our political system and corporate world, women in lower economic brackets will make less, work harder, sacrifice more, and ultimately face challenges at every turn, just to make ends meet. In *Feminism: Reinventing the F-Word*, Nadia Abushanab Higgins points out the ways in which our vocational world is still skewed to tilt men toward higher paying jobs. She says,

Most experts agree that workplace discrimination in the twenty-first century is real, but it's just one, relatively small factor in the wage gap. Work is still extremely gendered in the United States, and traditional men's jobs—such as engineering and construction work—pay a lot more than traditional women's jobs, including nursing and education. Even though women earn three bachelor of arts degrees for every two earned by men, they flock to "female" fields that pay less than "male" jobs. Compare the median annual wage for a kindergarten teacher, $53,000, to a computer programmer's at $74,000. Women's participation in high-paying STEM jobs is extremely low. Meanwhile, they comprise more than 94 percent of housekeepers, nannies and other domestic workers, which is about the lowest-paying, most undervalued work around. Women, disproportionately women of color, fill two-thirds of minimum wage jobs in the United States. They are more than twice as likely as men to rely on tips—which are unpredictable and sometimes very low—for a living, a predicament that triples any worker's risk for falling into poverty.[13]

These heavy consequences for women should be reason enough for people of faith to present a unified front for workplace equality. But if it's not, Ellen Bravo offers a more complex argument: inequality that operates in this systemic fashion negatively impacts not only women; it has real and tangible *consequences for children and men*, as well.

It's one thing to shake our heads at the statistics and lament that the world we live in is still so unbalanced for women. It's another thing entirely to acknowledge that our male-dominated worldview affects *all* of God's children adversely, and then to engage this problem in meaningful ways. There are plenty of things we can do individually to chip away at these systems and structures that continue to harm women and families. But the collective power of the body of Christ, when organized toward a common goal, can do so much more and have far greater transformative impact than any one of us alone. In far too many expressions of Christianity, however, the work of women's equality has been branded as just that: women's work. Further, it is culturally conflated with traditional feminism and all the baggage implied (as we've discussed in previous chapters).

Maybe this time and place in our shared story is precisely the right time for the people of God to reframe the conversation around women's justice issues, if for no other reason than the ways in which gender inequality contributes to systemic poverty. There is no chicken-and-egg question here. The unfair treatment of women doesn't just contribute to poverty; it is a direct source of the problem. Furthermore, systems of male dominance—namely, capitalism and big government—are the *direct beneficiaries* of women's continued suppression. With such large and far-reaching mechanisms actively engaged in preserving inequality, it is going to take other large bodies to undo the damage, to build a better world, and to tell a better story.

Is the church as we know it unified and equipped for this task? Hardly. But as people who claim to be followers of Christ, we have a moral imperative to try. You may be able to pull out a few proof texts to prevent a woman from speaking in church or to dictate how she should wear her hair. But Scripture contains more than 400 mentions of poverty and directives to care for the poor. Many of our churches dabble in addressing poverty in our communities. Maybe we serve at the food bank or help shelter the homeless. We can also advocate for a living wage in our home states. All of that is important.

But it's clear that we're never going to make any real progress in tackling the root causes of poverty unless we truly care about women and women's fair and equal treatment in the workplace. Correcting these imbalances improves not just women's well-being, but the well-being of the men, children, and elderly who may rely on their income.

UNEQUAL REPRESENTATION

It's nearly impossible to shift the workplace realities of women's lives in America, though, when women are so underrepresented in government. And, as Bravo points out, it's a vicious cycle with far more victims than beneficiaries. Creating meaningful change in these arenas is going to require leveraging more women's voices in every area of public life. As Marie Wilson of the White House Project notes,

> When it comes to women's leadership, we live in a land of deep resistance, with structural and emotional impediments burned into the cultures of our organizations, into our society, and into the psyches and expectations of both sexes. The problem is layered, as is the solution.
> That's why *numbers matter*. A single woman leader or a few women in a larger group are tokens. . . . Until there are enough diverse females in authority so that a chosen few are not expected to speak for an entire race or gender, those few will continue to carry the burden for us all.[14]

On the global stage right now, the United States ranks sixty-seventh in women's leadership. That puts us behind countries like Afghanistan and Cuba. In *Closing the Leadership Gap: Add Women, Change Everything,* Wilson argues that the lack of women's voices in public policy and global decision making is not unfair just to women; it skews the whole culture in which we live. She points out the ways in which women—if allowed to lead and employ the unique gifts and voices of women, rather than having to play by the rules of male-dominated culture—can begin to help reshape everything, from health care to world peace. Often, women who succeed in the corporate world do so by playing by the rules of the boys' club. Are they fierce? Are they badass? You bet. They have my undying admiration. But they have been invited, in many cases, "to join the patriarchy, not challenge it."[15]

The world's power structures, Wilson points out, are completely broken by the weight of male dominance. Adding more women's voices will shift that balance, not just in practical ways, but in deeper, more philosophical ways. It will enable men to make decisions based upon some of their gifts that are perceived as being more feminine qualities, like empathy and compassion. She says that "our business is no longer just gender equity, but the more sweeping industry of societal transformation."[16] There's nothing wrong with acknowledging that men and women do, in some ways, have different gifts and strengths. Women's influence could temper impulses to dominate with impulses to nurture, impulses to achieve and control with impulses to create and envision, and the impulse to overpower with the impulse toward relationship and community. Many of the world's power structures are inherently broken *because* of the void of women's voices in shaping them. In making room for a diversity of voices, insights, and experiences, we could infuse our systems of government, economy, education, and even religion with more just and balanced values.

That's a tall order. But if we truly want to live in a world that is more just and equitable—not just for women but for all people—we are called to build a world in which women's voices are valued as much as men's; where women are paid as much as men and are afforded equal opportunity for leadership and growth; and where women's vision is allowed to influence the larger narrative that we all inhabit. We also need multilayered approaches. For instance, to change the balance in those higher-paying STEM jobs, girls need to be supported in the math and sciences from a very young age. From the toys they play with at home to the ways teachers encourage and engage their interest, to the role models they are provided in the community, it will take a complex web of connections to really start to address the matter of the "leaky pipeline"—the phrase used for the systemic ways in which girls are often channeled away from these fields of study and vocation.

Leveraging more women into higher-paying positions is one approach. Meanwhile, there remains the overarching cultural baggage that literally devalues the jobs typically held by women. Recognizing that not all women are going to pursue careers in the sciences—whether because of lack of interest or lack of opportunity—we need to also address the matter of low wages in the fields where women do most of the work. We've noted already that childcare costs continue to escalate.

But actual childcare providers—who are mostly women—are not making more money. Where does that increase go? The cost increases go toward administrative and facility costs, rarely to the workers themselves. The same is true of nurses. More than 90 percent of nurses are women. But as healthcare costs climb (and climb, and climb), nurses continue to fight for fair wages and working conditions. The billions of dollars Americans spend for health care every year go, instead, to hospital administrators and the executives of major healthcare carrier corporations. The same is true of teachers. They continue to fight, in most states, for cost of living increases and to keep their basic pension benefits. Even when the economy is on the rise, teachers are told that the value of what they do doesn't merit a pay raise.

It's not that women are drawn to lower-wage jobs. It's that jobs typically held by women are literally valued less *because* they are considered "women's work."

STARTING WITH THE CHURCH

One of the first and most obvious ways the church can address inequality in the workplace is to tend to its own house—rather, houses of worship. In January 2016, the Religion News Service reported on the 2014 Bureau of Labor Statistics data on national median income of male and female clergy. This was the first time the BLS had been able to report those numbers, as they previously "could not make reliable estimates for women because of their relatively few numbers." According to the BLS figures, "women clergy earn 76 cents for each dollar earned by male clergy," a wage gap that is 4 to 7 cents greater than the estimated national gap.[17] If people of faith truly want to be part of the solution when it comes to unfair treatment of women in the workplace, the church itself has to learn to be a fair and equitable workplace. Churches need to learn how to negotiate gender-neutral personnel policies *with clear directives and expectations* for who gets paid how much, and for what.

Granted, clergy pay is all over the place, for men and women alike. With few denominational guidelines in place, other than recommendations or "best practices," many churches resort to a combination of local economy, church size, and pure guesswork when it comes to establishing clergy salaries.

If the practices for discerning salary range are haphazard, at best, then standards for clergy family leave are even less intentional and consistent. While women—and often men—in most of the developed world receive anywhere from three months to a year off, *with pay*, for the birth of a new child, the United States doesn't have any such federally mandated programs. American companies are free to develop their own policies, bound only by the Family and Medical Leave Act, which says, basically, you can take some time off *without* pay and probably still have your job, if you come back in whatever their definition of a timely fashion might be. Sadly, far too many churches err on the side of frugality and offer little paid leave.

The good news is that with more women serving in pastoral ministry, more congregations are thinking about how to prepare for their employees' life changes, both men and women. So it is a beginning. But if the church wants to lead any sort of social change, it needs to include women's equality in the conversation. To engage that issue, the church itself needs to be a better, more just employer.

In addition to doing right by its employees, the church has the power to model *for its members* a more just and life-giving approach to work-life balance and equal pay for all employees, regardless of gender. In my experience, it is often the high-ranking professionals in the congregation that help the church shape its administrative policies and operate as a functional organization. But shouldn't it be the other way around? When the church recognizes its influence on the wider community, by way of its influence on local employers who are connected with the congregation, this can go a long way toward shifting the culture in its view of working women.

This is the first point of engagement, because it is close to home. We can't tackle the bigger, more systemic issues if we don't have our own houses in order. But once we do, we can heed that call to step out in bigger, bolder, more prophetic ways and engage the systemic issues keeping many families in poverty.

Research shows a direct correlation between the number of women in a legislative body and the passage of bills benefitting women and children.[18] How much different would our political landscape look if we had an equal number of men and women serving in legislative roles? Or if we could just tip the scales a little closer to halfsies? It would completely change the conversation.

This is where it gets tricky, because congregations cannot directly engage in political action—for which I am thankful. I say this because I don't want the megachurch down the street to begin funneling millions of dollars, and yielding their rockstar preacher's pulpit, to whoever is the latest darling of the Pat Robertson crowd. I don't want my church, or yours, to become the mouthpiece of any political party or system, rather than proclaimers of the gospel.

But we can support local and state organizations that are nonpartisan and support policies benefiting women and children. If the church could organize around these causes with as much fervor as it has historically devoted to, say, the temperance movement—or "traditional marriage"—then it would be a whole new world out there. Furthermore, while congregations cannot engage in the election process for a party or candidate (nor would we want to), we *can*, and should, engage those who are currently in office. We can call our local and state representatives when there is a measure up for vote that will help (or hurt) women and children. We can tell them that our churches support a living wage and the enforcement of Title VII to ensure equal pay for women. We can write and make phone calls. We can even invite our local leaders to church events, to engage on another level, as long as we are sure to invite folks from both sides of the aisle.

When you get down to it, these issues should not be party-line issues. They are human issues, and, as such, they should be of primary concern for the community of faith. It's time to get political—not in the partisan sense but in the gospel sense, in the sense that Jesus was political. Jesus was very much aware that, while the empire was not his home, the way it operated touched every element of human life. Inevitably, any attempt to broach the topic of women's rights and equal pay in the faith community will bring critique that the church has gotten too political.

On the contrary, when it comes to these root causes of poverty so deeply entrenched in our systems, we have not been nearly political enough. Jesus might not have toed a party line, but he was about the business of humanity, the work of justice, and the deep and unwavering worth of every single person he encountered. If we think Jesus would not be advocating for the poorest among us—even the women—then we have been reading the gospel all wrong.

It wouldn't be the first time.

Questions for Reflection and Discussion

1. Do you think your employer has fair family-leave policies and offers equal pay for women? If not, what could you do to encourage them to change their practices?
2. How does the gospel imperative to care for the poor translate to equal pay for women? What other systemic-justice issues might also be addressed in eliminating the wage gap?
3. Can you think of a time when you witnessed a workplace injustice against a woman? Or experienced one yourself? How can the community of faith address these systems that enable unfair treatment of women?

7

Stop Telling Me to Smile: Double Standards and Demanding Routines

Here's what women do, most mornings in the developed world: shower (possibly after a workout); put on makeup of varying degrees, based on personal preference; put on underwear and a bra—possibly a terrible bra that will dig into your ribs all day long, and rub and chafe and just generally squeeze your insides—and *possibly* some other supporting garment; put on clothing, which somebody (probably you) had to purchase, launder, *iron*(??), and arrange into a coordinating outfit; add appropriate shoes, many of which, for professional women, are super uncomfortable and cost a fortune. There is probably need of some appliance usage in here, as well—hair dryer, straightening iron, curling iron, curlers, and so on. Add product. Maybe multiple products.

Add to this the every-few-days shaving of the legs, wherein we ironically try to *remove* hair, before we go to work on managing the hair atop the head; the occasional manicure or pedicure situation; skincare regimen (morning and evening!); the monthly or semimonthly trip to the stylist to take care of the hair and eyebrow business; perhaps an every-few-weeks need to cover gray roots (if you're into that) either at the salon or out of the $9 box.

Now, add up the time and energy all that takes, and then factor in the expense of all the toiletries and services involved.

You may or may not do all this while simultaneously getting children dressed, checking homework, packing lunches, and generally wrangling the world for the school drop-off routine.

We could book a trip to Hawaii for what we spend looking vaguely presentable every day. I say, book it. Because this. Shit. Is. *Exhausting*.

This is why dry shampoo has been a game-changer for all of womankind. This is also why I refuse to wear uncomfortable shoes. I will wear makeup; I will wear a bra out of the necessities of physics; I will cover up my gray roots, just because I've not quite made peace with being gray before I hit forty; I will do many things to keep up with the ridiculous beauty standards that television, magazines, *and apparently Scripture* have put upon us. But, God as my witness, I will have comfortable feet while I do it.

You know what my husband does every morning? He takes a shower. He shaves. Brushes his teeth. And he's out. He looks fine. He looks professional. His whole outfit cost less than one pair of my (mostly comfortable) shoes.

He also probably slept about nine hours last night. Me, I'm more like Leslie Knope, from *Parks and Recreation*, who says, "I just slept seven hours—which is twice as long as I usually sleep, so I'm a little disoriented."

Double standards are nothing new. Let's talk for a moment about Eve and that apple. (Which was not really an apple, but that's neither here nor there.) Whatever kind of exotic Middle Eastern fruit the writer of Genesis may have had in mind, that tree right there is the root of the fruits of patriarchy—and in particular the double standards around beauty, sexuality, and femininity that plague us to this day.

First of all, the Hebrew word *adam*—pronounced as ah-dahm and typically translated as a proper name, Adam—is actually a gender-neutral word. The distinction between male and female emerges only when a second being is created. Once the two become one being in marriage, those distinctions fall away.[1] Interestingly enough, that genderless state of being is also how many in the early church viewed baptism: as something that made all distinctions and boundaries fall away, so that all were one/equal in the Spirit. (Don't get too excited; church fathers and a couple of popes effectively wipe that from the narrative later.)

In any case, the first two created humans were on a far more equal footing than later readings would have us believe. The word *ezer*, which we translate as "helper," has also been manipulated to make it sound as though Eve was created for the sole purpose of serving Adam as her master. In fact, the word actually means something more like a partner. It's meant to indicate a mutually beneficial relationship—more to the point, a relationship that was beneficial for all of creation, as the two cared for the earth together as stewards.[2]

Fast forward beyond the honeymoon stage, and we come to the episode that has really and truly screwed women for all time: that fruit tree. Again, when we read this story as a too-literal accounting of something that happened—as opposed to a narrative employed to help humans make sense of their world and identity—Eve appears as a caricature, a femme fatale whose one mission in life was to entice a hapless man to sin. And it's all downhill from there.

The Christian tradition has used that singular moment as defense for subjugating women, for keeping them silent, for keeping them covered up, and—in extreme cases—for abusing women as a means of "discipline." Because after all, if God saw fit to punish women in childbirth for this episode, then shouldn't men go about punishing them further? Never mind the fact that God had a whole separate litany of punishments for the menfolk. That tends to get overlooked in the interest of subverting womankind for all of history.

Surely we can see the toxic ripples of that reading. We can also see the ways in which a patriarchal culture superimposed its own values on the legend.

Even in the most literal reading of Scripture, the text in no way creates that image of Eve as temptress. Barbara J.

MacHaffie writes, "Nowhere in the story does the woman seduce or entice the man. The verb 'to seduce' or 'to deceive' is used only in connection with the serpent's activities. Nowhere does the story say that the woman tempted the man or used wicked persuasion. The text simply says, 'She gave some to her husband and he ate.'"[3]

Yes, God comes down, mad as hell, but *even God Herself does not say that Eve is being too sexy.* That is not the complaint. The problem is that these first two creatures—both of them—ate from a tree of knowledge that would make them more like God. It would open their eyes to the distinctions of good and evil, taking them from a pure state to a fallen one. In essence, they wanted to know too much. And it changed everything.

But really, that's it? Did that verse create the whole world of male dominance and all the suffering that implies?

The image of Eve as a temptress—the image that has perpetuated to this day a far-reaching mistrust of women's bodies, voices, and abilities—is pure fiction. But it's an effective fiction when used as a tool of manipulation and control. Of course, Eve is not the only biblical woman to get a bad rap.

Both Christian and secular historians have long been obsessed with Mary Magdalene. Who was she? What did she look like? How well did Jesus "know" her? What was her role in the Jesus movement? Well, scholars and theologians have been digging around to answer that forever. But around the fourth century, some prominent theologians conflated stories of Mary Magdalene with stories of other women in the Gospels: Mary of Bethany; the prostitute who wept at Jesus' feet; and maybe some of the other Marys.[4] The women's stories were intentionally conflated, effectively painting Mary Magdalene—disciple, friend, and first preacher—as a whore.

Perfect.

By the sixth century, "prostitute" was widely accepted as the common narrative and identity of this powerful, mysterious woman. As a narrative device, I suppose this works well to display the benevolence and transformative powers of Jesus.

But as for honoring the narrative of a strong woman in our faith history, and recognizing her as the leader she was? It kind of blows. Somewhere around the year 591 Pope Gregory the Great conveniently used this narrative of Mary as whore to justify locking women out of the clergy.[5] Here we are, hundreds of years later, still fighting the consequences. In her book *Holy Misogyny*, April D. DeConick notes:

> By reframing certain elements of her story and inserting new elements within it, her prominence is marginalized or replaced by the male heroes and leaders of the movement when the gospels were written. This remodeling of Mary's traditional story occurred at a time when women's roles in some of the churches were being called into question because of the social and cultural implications of their leadership.[6]

You get the gist. Sounds familiar, doesn't it?

MIXED SIGNALS

Clearly, the church has always had a fraught relationship with women's bodies. Our physical frames are both danger and delight; threat and comfort; forbidden fruit, which is super arousing, and modest virtue, which is to be applauded—but, let's face it, is not very sexy. Heck, one of the very first double standards of feminine beauty and shame is right there in Paul's epistles, for anybody with eyes to see. A woman is to keep her head covered, because of virtue and modesty, but she is not to cut her hair, because her hair is her glory. Why cover it up if it's her glory? Why make her grow it out and carry that heavy, hot mess around on her neck if it's just going to be covered up?

This world of conflicting messages is not just a thing of ancient culture. We are saturated with similar tensions and contradictions to this day—which amounts to a world of discomfort, stress, and expense for women everywhere.

It's not just about what we wear. Sometimes it's about our face.

For instance, men frequently approach women they don't know and tell them to smile. Yes, this is a thing. On the surface, it is a casual, passing friendliness. It's maybe a way of engaging small talk (wanted or otherwise) or a way of saying, "Hey, I notice you, and your face doesn't look happy."

If a man I don't know tells me to smile, what he's essentially telling me is not just that I should be happy, but that I should be *nice*, that my face should look a certain way in order to be pleasing to him or to the world in general. First, maybe this is just my face. Second, it is not my job to look—or *be*—pleasant for anybody else.

Artist Tatyana Fazlalizadeh launched "Stop Telling Women to Smile," a street campaign and website intended to address gender-based harassment. As writer and activist Bené Viera puts it,

> Men tell women to smile because society conditions men to think we exist for the male gaze and for their pleasure. Men are socialized to believe they have control over women's bodies. This results in them giving unsolicited instructions on how we should look, think, and act. Essentially what a man is saying when he tells a woman—one he doesn't even know—to smile, is that his wants outweigh her own autonomy over how she exists in the world.[7]

Among people who don't identify with feminism, there lives a misperception that feminists are angry all the time. The "Don't tell me to smile" movement, however subtle, may contribute to that stereotype, and not in a good way. At the same time, this conversation isn't just about smiling or not smiling. It is about a whole culture of male domination, in which men are raised, conditioned, and programmed to feel—and sometimes exert—a sense of ownership and control over women's bodies. This happens in small and large ways every day. If women don't feel like smiling sometimes, this is a big fat part of why. I'm not saying we all go around seething and mad at the world every day . . . but man, it is a lot sometimes. Between the bras and the heels and the added weight of ridiculous double standards, that stuff gets heavy.

Anyway, maybe this is just my face. This brings us to *Resting Bitch Face*.

Yes, this is also a thing now. I know some women who will cheerfully admit that they have one: a face that, when not actively smiling, laughing, or talking, looks like a firestorm brewing and scares away men—not to mention small children and woodland creatures. I explained Resting Bitch Face to my grandmother recently, when we were watching some sporting event on television and she mentioned that a woman on the sidelines looked really mad about something. "No," I said, "maybe she just has . . ." I will always remember how she cackled when I told her what that meant.

But it's complicated. Because, other than maybe being a nice joke with my Mamaw, Resting Bitch Face is (1) another opportunity for the world to call women bitches, and (2) one more way by which to measure a woman's appearance. Is it happy enough? Docile and compliant enough? Pleasant and ready to put at ease all who come into her path?

Women are not put on this earth just to be pleasant and put people at ease. Maybe I don't want you to feel at ease about judging or critiquing my appearance. Maybe my general expression is not an invitation for a stranger to comment on the general looks of me—because the entitlement to comment on a woman's expression is directly related to entitlement to women's bodies and personal space.

Here are some things that happened to me, all in one day. This one day is by no means the norm, nor is it meant to be an exhaustive list of the kinds of intrusion women endure daily. (For that, read *Everyday Sexism,* as I mentioned in chapter 1.) It just happened to be a weird day for interactions with men, and I think it captures more than a glimpse of most women's experience.

First, a man called me a fascist bitch on Twitter. I'm a blogger and a woman who has the nerve to say things. So the name-calling is nothing new.

Then an elderly funeral director told me that I'd sure be cute . . . if I had red hair. (Read: I find your purple hair unbefitting a proper lady. Also, I think you are twelve years old, and women should not be ministers.)

Then another man from the same funeral home (honestly, I have some rotten luck with funeral directors) rubbed all up and down my arm. A light touch on the shoulder might have been appropriate in this context, because I was talking to someone else and he needed to interrupt us for a moment to ask me a quick question. But he did not lightly touch my shoulder. He gave my arm and shoulder a full-on rub down. On bare skin, no less, as I had just taken off my jacket and was wearing a sleeveless top.

I want you to picture a middle-aged, male funeral director walking up to a male pastor—whom he has just met for the first time—at the conclusion of a funeral service and rubbing all up and down his arm while addressing him about a professional matter. That would be absurd!

Right.

Then the same day—I'm not even joking—a stranger in Panera stopped me and proceeded to rub patronizingly all up and down my back while he told me, in hushed tones, that the tag was sticking out the back of my shirt. "I'm sorry, *do I know you?*"

You know the best part? This guy was sitting and talking with another guy. And from overhearing their conversation, I learned that they were both ministers.

These are totally different things. But they are also exactly the same.

These are anecdotal episodes. But they are also the universal experience of womanhood. Men think our bodies are theirs, because everything about our culture—even, and especially, in church—tells them that is true.

As different as these exchanges seemed at the time—the menacingly hostile troll, the harmless funeral director, the arm rubber, the tag fixer—these events also have a lot in common, primarily the frequency with which they occur. Yes, all of these things happened in one (very strange) day; but that doesn't make that day extraordinary. I deal with name-calling from strangers, uninvited comments on my appearance—plus vaguely inappropriate touching—on a regular basis.

So does every other woman you know. This is the same world in which journalist Erin Andrews filed charges against a stalker and the hotel in which she was spied on; and was slut-shamed in a court of law, and accused of using the stalker incident to get attention and promote her public profile. This is the world in which more than half of recent seminary graduates are women; but the rate of women serving as lead and solo pastors hovers between 10 and 15 percent. (Research in this area is variable and does not account for church size. If we were counting only moderate to large congregations, the percentage would be much lower.)

This is also the same world in which we teach our daughters to dress modestly, avoid dark alleyways, and in a thousand other ways navigate the land mines of rape culture. Yet we have not managed to teach our boys that no means no. Girls are expected to be beautiful, even sexy at younger and younger ages (is it just me, or do they make padded bikini tops for toddlers these days?). At the same time, we find a thousand ways a day to tell girls their bodies are shameful, an invitation for judgment, and in so many ways just plain problematic. This is the world we live in, the world that says if you are wearing a long skirt and high neckline, you're a prude, but if you are wearing spaghetti straps, you are probably a slut.

DRESSING THE PART

When I was in high school youth group, we used to go to a big outdoor Christian music festival called Ichthus. It was in a big field in a small town in Kentucky, and thousands of youth from all over the country would flock there to camp and, you know, rock out to "Jesus Freak," have fellowship, and generally jam to some good Christian rock. (I know. Oxymoron.) I remember one year when one of the performers onstage—they were always taking a break in the concert for a literal come-to-Jesus moment—took his preaching moment to caution all the "young ladies" out there about the clothing they would choose to wear this weekend. He said we needed to remember that we were "God's daughters," that we deserved to be treated with respect (yes, OK, fine), and then he said, "You wouldn't want something that you wear to cause someone else to stumble" ("stumble" being teenage pop-Christian code for "sin"). He was generally referring to short shorts and shoulder-revealing tank tops. We would not want too much of our skin to be the reason for some poor boy's fall into . . . what, puberty?

Even as a sixteen-year-old, I knew that was some kind of BS. Did I mention we were *camping*? Most years it rained, turning this field into one giant mud pit. There were no showers. Everyone was filthy. We were literally kids on a camping trip—playing outside, having fun, singing Jesus songs. Yet this Christian performer was *super* concerned about my tank top. As though a small glimpse of my shoulder might bring something dirty and shameful into this otherwise holy event. Where all the boys, of course, were thinking nothing but pure thoughts, as always.

Nope. Nossir. Come to think about it, that might be the moment I decided to be a tank-top-wearing feminist.

This is the same kind of thinking that leads the defending attorney in a rape trial to ask the victim, "What were you wearing?" As though the men around us cannot be held responsible for their actions if we were stupid enough to flash some thigh. It's a toxic line of reason, dangerous to men and women alike. It is also fraught with the double standards of purity culture, in which women are expected to be *just* sexy enough . . . without giving too much away.

Which is it? Are we too much, or not enough? Are we too revealing, or too prudish? Are we too sexy, or not pretty enough? Are we your mother, your mistress, or your daughter? These are impossible lines to walk each day. No wonder we aren't smiling.

This is just the world we live in. Right?

Somehow, the liturgical repetition of that truth doesn't make us feel better about its reality. It may be time for a new mantra.

The trouble is, at the personal, day-to-day level, most of the time, it's easy enough to shrug off. It's easy enough to block the troll, laugh off the grandfatherly comment, or sidestep the "friendly" rubdown that should have been a light tap on the arm. In the moment, it feels like the professional thing to do— the most gracious, the most hospitable, the least likely to lead to ugly confrontation.

The truth is that we delete/laugh/sidestep because it's *easier*. It's the easiest way to be a woman in "the world we live in." But the world in which we choose to ignore or blow off the subtle expressions of misogyny is the same world that enables—even encourages—the systemic, more harmful ones.

We are allowed to be pissed about this.

We are allowed to get angry that women's bodies are considered deeply, inherently controversial—not controversial just in the political/ideological sense regarding reproductive rights and health care. Apparently, there is *fundamentally* something offensive and confusing about curves, cleavage, and knees. And I guess, now, bones?

We hear stories like this every day. This one happened to make the news because the mother pitched an epic fit and wrote an amazing letter that went viral when her daughter, a student at a Kentucky high school, was sent home for wearing a top that was very, very revealing . . . of her collar bones.[8] Literally, the complaint was that you could see her collar bones. Go try on every shirt in your closet and see how many reveal a hint of clavicle. Fellas too! We'll wait.

Meanwhile, around the same time, the Missouri legislature was dealing with an embarrassing sexual harassment suit; an intern said that one of the legislators made inappropriate remarks and advances toward her. How did they deal with it, in the upper echelons of state government? Well, they figured that maybe a stricter dress code would cut down on the drama—a dress code *for the women,* that is.

108   RESIST AND PERSIST

Our bodies are not like a tax law, to be voted yes or no upon. All this controversy is confounding. Our bodies exist. We walk around in them. We are kind of attached to them.

How other people choose to act in proximity of a breast— or a collar bone, or a knee—is distinctly not our problem.

Yes, there are appropriate ways to dress for a professional setting; yes, maybe there are a few things that should probably not be worn to school. But since those boundaries are ambiguous and situational, the people in charge of defining them often err on the side of *just cover it up and make it easier for us.* The fact is that most dress codes in a school, work, or government environment are a list of standards that apply almost *exclusively to women.*

The "cover it up" approach implies a couple of things that are problematic for both men and women. Men should be offended by the message that they are animals who cannot control their urge to hump every lamp post that looks like a woman's leg. I have not found this to be true of (most) men, and it is pretty insulting to (most) of their intelligence that I might need to wear a burka so that they can focus on their math homework or sales presentation.

Furthermore, woven into the basic dress code is the implication that women need to hide their business in order to *do* business. Every time we tell a girl, no matter how old she is, that it's her responsibility to dress modestly so that she does not tempt a boy to behave badly, we reinforce the notion that a man is entitled to an opinion on her body . . . closely followed by the memo that a man is entitled to articulate that opinion . . . which points to the nearby truth that a man is entitled to her personal space.

We are frighteningly aware: that last part is *more than implied* in our cultural reality.

As a woman, I struggle to dress myself, to find that balance between function and fashion; between what is comfortable and what is grown-up work clothes; between what is flattering and what is going to draw unwanted comments from the peanut gallery. It is way more complicated than it needs to be.

As a mother of a daughter, I also struggle to find, and model, good boundaries. I see girls walking to high school in shorts that are really denim panties, and I think, *"My kid would not be let out of the house in that."* My inner Tim Gunn regularly shouts, *"Leggings aren't pants!"* And I fight the urge to approach women wearing four-inch stilettos and say, "Sister, you are ruining your feet. And your knees. And who's it for?" If they said, "I wear them for *me,* because they make me feel beautiful and strong!" then I would say, "OK then." (But I may or may not believe them, because how strong can you feel in that misery?) Here's the thing though: I'm not the boss of other people's feet—or legs or ass cheeks, for that matter. So I keep my comments to myself. And men should do the same.

Having good boundaries for ourselves, expecting professionalism in the workplace, and even wanting to teach our daughters about modesty and *good taste* are not the same things as policing women's bodies in official, systemic ways. This really comes back to the issue of *trusting women.* We need to trust women to clothe themselves, to carry themselves, to be in charge of their own personal space. We've gone from days when women weren't allowed to wear pants—when they were literally arrested in the streets if they stepped outside not wearing a dress or skirt—to the days when girls go to school in shorts that barely cover anything that matters. The span of time between these two sets of expectations is minimal, at best. Our expectations of women's dress and appearance are constantly changing, and it seems that, no matter the time or place, there is a deep sense of shame surrounding the appearance and coverage (or lack thereof) of women's bodies.

So maybe it's time to change the conversation.

When the time comes for me to say to my daughter, "No, ma'am, you are not wearing those shorts to school," it will not have anything to do with boys. It will not be "because you are 'asking for it'" or "because you will lure some poor boy into sin." Gag me. If I tell my daughter to cover up her booty, it will be because I want for *her* to value herself for more than just the skin she's in. I want her to understand that her body belongs to her, and that some parts of it are not to be shared with the public at large. *Not because the parts are shameful,* but because maybe it makes you forget—especially when you are young—that the world around you is not entitled to *all* of you. Also, maybe I just want her to avoid being tacky. But mostly, I want her to think about how she presents herself to the world, as the whole and unique person she is, not just as a body or the parts of the body that draw the most attention. I want her to be aware of how patriarchy has "dressed" women, forever—even when it feels as if we are making our own choices.

Believe it or not, I'm hopeful. Because this conversation is, finally, shifting.

In Kentucky, after that student's mother wrote her epic missive to the principal, she started a movement; and the school is now reassessing its draconian standards, *with a group of students* serving as leaders in the conversation.

The Missouri legislature reconsidered its proposal as well.[9] They figured that perhaps instead of putting the female interns in hazmat suits, what we need to do is expect that our elected officials should maybe learn to keep it in their pants.

A school in Illinois recently revealed its new dress code. It is based on what they call a "body positive" philosophy.[10] While it does ban shirts that include profane or hateful messaging, it basically says that students can all wear what makes them comfortable. Full stop. Amazing.

I'd call this progress. Slow but steady.

Meanwhile, I wish the fashion industry would take a cue from that school district when it decides what women are going to wear to work and buy in stores this season. Think about it. Shoes that are basically stilts; bras that are basically corsets; Spanx, which are *actual corsets*; swimsuits with "control panels" and yoga pants with "tummy control."

Control is the patriarchy's bottom line: control our bodies; control the space in which we can live, work, and just *be*; control the roles we can assume, the voices we are allowed, the face we make in public. It's all about control. We are even led to want to control and contain our own figures—Spanx, underwires, control-top pantyhose. It is all about holding in and manipulating what nature gave us for our own.

It's no wonder if we are exhausted, sisters. It's OK to admit it. We are *tired*, tired of this march to perfection, tired of these triple-and-quadruple-fraught standards, tired of always being too much for somebody and not nearly enough for everyone else. Can we find a way to rest from this nonsense together? Meanwhile, fellas . . . we need you to get our backs here, OK? Because we are wore-slick-out (as folks say down home in the holler, where I'm from). We need you to respect personal space; to understand when we aren't smiling sometimes; to step in and say, "Back off," when you see other dudes invading our space; to acknowledge the work that we put our bodies through every day; to understand what it is like to walk a mile in our super-awkward shoes. All of this would go a long, long way to help unwind some of the literal bondage that is wound around our waking days.

Meanwhile, the church itself has helped put some of this underwire and Spandex bondage in place, and can help loose it, on-earth-as-it-is-in-heaven. These are systemic things we're trying to unwind here—not in a "fight your legislature" kind of way, but in more deeply encultured and philosophical kinds of ways.

Most simply and most importantly, stop teaching garbage theology about Eve and original sin. Her lady parts were not the downfall of humankind; so just stop that narrative in its tracks. Dig a little deeper and talk about original sin as an act of treading too close to the holy; as a boundary-crossing that men and women shared equally and that had little to do with fruit or anybody's uterus.

Churches—and camps, parachurch organizations, Christian events, and so on—should also revisit any dress-code policies that they employ for youth and children. That "you don't want to cause your brothers to stumble" thing is still going strong. At our local church camp, which is pretty progressive, in the grand scheme of things, my eight-year-old daughter was told her tankini was unacceptable at the camp pool. A tankini. She's eight. What is the message there? That there is something inherently shameful or threatening about her belly button? Even the seminary I attended had a best-practices kind of thing for wardrobe, and every single point of info in that thing applied only to women. Are our policies and expectations in church and related gatherings geared toward controlling and/or shaming girl's bodies, and deflecting the men's poor behavior onto the woman's hem or neckline? If so, we are doing it wrong.

This is not just about what we *don't* teach. As is so often the case, the modern church is often good at articulating what we don't believe, but we are often not equipped with a counter-narrative that is more life-giving. Rather than just rejecting a certain biased reading of Scripture, we need to develop a faithful teaching of gender and worth that is rooted in a healthy theology of embodiment. Such a consistent message of equality and worthiness will empower women and girls to own their own space—by choosing what they wear, how they cover (or don't) their own bodies, and what expression they wear on their face. It's about treating sex as a sacred mystery to explore with reverence, not as a threat hiding around the corner in the form of some dangerous woman. It's a long way from Eve and her apple to this place of just and balanced gender equity. But if we hold all this tension lightly, and engage these conversations with care, then we can begin to loose all the bondage around our women's hearts—and boobs and thighs and hips and stomachs, and . . .

Questions for Reflection and Discussion

1. Can you think of a time when you were told your clothing was not appropriate? If this discussion is happening in mixed company, there is probably some disparity of experience here across gender lines. Discuss.

2. What teachings, policies, or practices might your faith community or organization need to revisit to remove messages of shame or control?
3. How might we reenvision the Creation story, particularly the part about Eve in the garden, to teach a theology of sacred embodiment instead of sin and shame?

8

The New Frontier: Silencing Women, One Tweet at a Time

Our founding mothers didn't exactly have to deal with limiting their kids' screen time or policing their online acquaintances. They didn't have to worry about creating a public profile and upholding a certain image. Nobody tweeted threats to Abigail Adams when she asked her husband to give women the vote. Nobody Instagrammed graphic pictures to slut-shame Dolley Madison when she accidentally showed an ankle.

Women in early waves of feminism didn't have to worry about their online presence either. Susan B. Anthony and Elizabeth Cady Stanton didn't have to establish a social media platform to work for women's suffrage. But neither did they have to endure a constant onslaught of threats, harassment, and name-calling that visible and vocal women face today.

Even in the 1960s and 1970s, when the fight for women's equality was at its most heated and women endured all manner of overt discrimination in the public sphere, they did not have to deal with this particular challenge. Today we find ourselves in uncharted territory. On the one hand, the evolution of digital media, the effortless sharing of information, and our constant state of connectedness has created unprecedented opportunity to amplify women's voices in politics, entertainment, and industry. Yet social media has also unleashed a new kind of monster that women must fight at every turn when they attempt to speak out. This monster is loud and fearless and large, and it seems no set of potential consequences will stop it in its tracks. Behold, the age of the Internet troll.

Internet trolls are real; they are scary; and more often than not, they go after the women. Any woman with any sort of public presence these days can attest to the real and present shadow of web trolls. From bullying to actual physical threats, this brand of misogyny is a new frontier facing women— especially strong, vocal women.

This trend is not about any one public figure, but Donald Trump has modeled a whole new dimension of online harassment of women. While he has been openly harassing women based on their looks since long before he came onto the political scene, his range of influence grew to alarming proportions once he became the GOP frontrunner in the 2016 campaign. And as president he opened a portal to a whole new dimension, revealing how loudly and widely it is still accepted, in this day and age, to attack a woman for her looks, her opinions, or just her nerve to generally be around.

During an early presidential debate, facilitator Megyn Kelly questioned then-candidate Trump about some of his previous remarks about women. Feeling he was unfairly targeted by the challenging question (which would become a trend in his engagement with the media in general), he shot back with a firestorm of tweets (which would also become a trend of his presidency). In this cluster of statements, he called Kelly— among other things—a "lightweight," a "bimbo," and "average in so many ways." He also said in a later interview that she was "bleeding out of her eyes . . . bleeding out of her whatever." That original statement, though confounding and inappropriate at the time, was not nearly as concerning as what followed.

Internet trolls travel in packs. They feed off of each other, like the women-hating parasites that they are. Where yesterday there was one, today there are a hundred. Tomorrow there will be 10,000.

Trump's name-calling of Kelly, though in poor taste, seemed harmless enough at first—the stuff of reality-television sensationalism (which, isn't it all these days?). But what he effectively did with his disparaging words was issue an all-call to misogynistic bullies everywhere. "Now is our time to shine, fellas!" he said with the 140-character bat signal. "Let her have it!"

Boy, did they ever! Over the next few weeks, Kelly received threats of rape, threats of death, even threats against her family. She had to start traveling with bodyguards.

It was open season on women in the media—or, it would seem, women in general.

The pattern went on like this. Women who were running for office in 2016, in both parties, experienced an unprecedented level of online threats, name-calling, body shaming, and general public animosity. Not necessarily from their political opponents, or even relative to their political views, but from men who felt emboldened by the public displays of misogyny that continued to spin out from a certain Twitter account.

As a blogger during that time, I frequently commented on this state of affairs. So when the tapes emerged in which Trump bragged he could "grab women by the . . ."—well, you know—and his defenders rushed to embrace the "locker room" and "all men talk like that" line of reasoning, I realized that in some people's worlds that is true. I was deeply saddened and angered by that reality.

So I went to Twitter myself. And I said this: "If you think all men talk like that, then might I suggest an upgrade of the men in your life."

That statement was retweeted more than ten thousand times, which means it made its way beyond the boundaries of my usual like-minded-reader circle. There is nothing profane or remotely offensive in this statement, nothing in line with party politics (because leaders on both sides of the aisle were openly appalled by his behavior—though some not quite vocally enough). There is no implication that all men are pigs. In fact, I am clearly suggesting that there are wonderful men out there—better men, stronger men, smarter men, who treat women with dignity. I was suggesting to all the ladies out there that, if they were buying the defense that "all men" behave this way, then I have good news! There is life out there! Ditch the loser and come see for yourself.

You would have thought I was suggesting that women receive equal pay or something absurd like that. Because the Internet lost its dang mind.

After that Tweet, I had to turn off all the social-media notifications on my phone. And I haven't turned them back on since, because in just the first hour after hitting "send" on that statement, I was called

Ignorant

Idiot

"Woman"

Sweetheart

FemiNazi

Hysterical Loon

Bitch

I also was told to shut up. Which is a typical message received by women who try to say things. There were also suggestions about my obvious lack of sexual opportunity/experience/ enjoyment, if no man has ever talked to me like that before. It was suggested that my Friday night involved nine cats and a tub of ice cream. It went on like that for a while.

At some point, I went to bed. I woke up the next morning to an even longer list of new titles I can add to my resume. I blocked the guy who called me a bitch. I also blocked a guy whose Twitter handle is @TwatSlayer (whose mother, I'm sure, is so proud of her baby boy).

But this is not all. The underlying message of all these tweets was an insistence that, yes, all men *do* talk like that—which makes it OK, which makes me an ignorant, hysterical female for expecting otherwise. Meanwhile—and here's where it gets really confounding—the *men* who commented in agreement or support of me were called names as well. Names like:

Pussies

Not real men

Gay

Lapdogs

And my favorite, "whimps" (Note: sexist trolls *love* it when you correct their spelling or grammar. Try it sometime.)

So there is another whole layer of misogyny here, in that *men* who support women are also disregarded, shamed, and emasculated, as though you can't be a real man unless you, too, hate women. There's also a very hetero-normative worldview in all of this, with the implication that men who are gay are *just as bad as women*—which, in a misogynistic culture, is of course the worst thing you can possibly be. That not-so-subtle messaging reflects how hard patriarchy works to preserve itself in the most overt and disgusting ways.

Of course, this is just one example of how one vocal misogynist emboldens and empowers a slew of others, while a man voicing support of women invites the ire of his peers. This is a pattern that reaches far beyond the realm of social media. Donald Trump is not the only public figure out there who diminishes women in this way. But given the size and scope of his platform, and his knack for drumming up a following, his behavior toward women is harmful on a much larger scale. (It seems as though his platform should have been "making misogyny great again.") In fact, some have said his social media habits openly defy Twitter's actual harassment policy: "You may not promote violence against or directly attack or threaten other people on the basis of race, ethnicity, national origin, sexual orientation, gender, gender identity, religious affiliation, age, disability, or disease."

It is widely known that Twitter has a hard time enforcing these community guidelines. When you have a Troll-in-Chief modeling the behavior, how can anyone hope to rein in the hordes of people who feel emboldened to do likewise?

I AIN'T AFRAID OF NO TROLLS

I shared my own experience of online harassment, knowing that it is small compared to that of women who have larger platforms, and knowing that my online experience as a white woman is nothing compared to that of women of color.

For an extremely high-profile example, take what happened to SNL's Leslie Jones after the release of the all-women version of *Ghostbusters*. Talk about the Internet losing its mind. The very thought that women had hijacked one of the greatest bro movies of all time was too much for some. Add to the mix a woman of color, and it was completely unacceptable.

To be clear, the movie itself was in no way controversial. It was *Ghostbusters,* of all things! And the women who made the movie were not out beating drums for equality or making political commentary of any kind. They were just women who had the gall to show up in a public space. That is too much for some people.

Leslie Jones did not one thing to instigate a Twitter tirade from thousands of angry white men. She was just there, appearing on screen, being a black woman with a voice. It was enough to fill people with rage.

The ugliness all started with a review in a Breitbart publication. Milo Yiannopoulos, alt-right darling and professional troll, posted a negative review of *Ghostbusters* on Breitbart, referencing Jones's "flat-as-a-pancake black stylings."[1] Some of his followers and like-minded bros started trolling Jones with sexist and racist comments and ugly memes. What really amped things up was when Yiannopoulos began tweeting at

Jones directly—while sharing fake tweets pretending to actually *be* her. So he effectively bullied her and stole her identity all at once—different tactics, but both attempts to silence a woman of color with a strong public profile. It was really just all downhill from there.

As the threats and slurs amped up, Jones appealed to Twitter multiple times for intervention. (Twitter, meanwhile, has been accused on more than one occasion of being more responsive to complaints from white women than from women of color.) When they didn't respond in a timely fashion, she ultimately suspended her account and temporarily left the platform.

The good news is that Yiannopoulos had his account suspended too—and not by choice. Twitter finally got it together and banished him. But his message was out there, and had been amplified to something far greater than a single user's thread.

While the story of a movie star having to leave social media does not sound tragic, on the surface—I mean, she is Leslie Freaking Jones; she will be OK—this episode actually offers some deeply discouraging commentary on the way in which many people react to women's advancement. For all the progress we have made since the days of our grandmothers (and even our mothers), there is still widespread resistance out there when it comes to including women—especially minority women—as equal voice and presence in pop culture.

Every woman author/blogger/speaker I know has experienced at least some measure of online harassment. Every woman in politics has experienced the same. Really, to be in politics these days, you *have* to develop an online media presence. And the more presence, voice, and visibility a woman has, the more backlash she can expect to endure.

We often refer to this kind of behavior as the last breath of patriarchy, the desperate death cry of a system and worldview that is on its way out. I'd like to believe that is true. Some days I'm hopeful that it might be true. But at other times, it seems that this death cry has been a sustained wail for centuries now, as every small step for womankind creates some giant leap for misogyny, and every measure of development and progress for women issues a new invitation for repression. Sexist jerks have to get more creative now to operate within the framework of the law and polite society. But they just keep coming, don't they?

Situations like the ones with Leslie Jones and Megyn Kelly are not isolated incidents. They are all about one thing: power. When a group of men—even if they do not speak for all men—go about squeezing a woman's voice out of the public sphere, they are working hard to diminish all women as whole people. When men attack female entertainers, they are resisting feminine influence on the shaping of art and culture. When men attack female reporters and bloggers, they are attempting to limit women's voices from our shared narrative. The goal is to discourage women from taking up space in all the major areas of public life; and keeping women out of politics, religion, commerce, and even entertainment is a pretty effective way of maintaining a masculine status quo. It is also a roundabout way of resurrecting (or sustaining) that old cult of ideal womanhood, where women were revered but kept on a pretty short leash, relegated to the spheres of home and childrearing.

While that may be a truly satisfying path for some women, what's toxic are the patterns by which women continue to be discouraged, or even barred, from wading into other arenas. These tactics are not always effective, which is why women have made gradual progress over the centuries. Still, the numbers don't lie: the number of women in political office, high-powered corporate jobs, and even directing movies and television shows, remains low compared to the number of men doing those same jobs. So our broader culture is shaped powerfully by men's voices, vision, and worldview.

AN OLD STORY ON A NEW STAGE

The Internet may be a new horizon, a new medium for silencing women, but the practice of diminishing women's stories is a time-honored tradition. This is why a man can brag about his aggressive and demeaning treatment of women and still get elected as leader of the free world.

It's all part of the same destructive pattern, built firmly upon the notion that women—their voices, their experiences, their very lives—just don't matter as much as men do. It's the narrative that women are meant to be the helpers, the supporting actresses, the keepers of home and the wranglers of the young, and possibly teachers in Sunday school (only for children or other women, of course). But in the more visibly world-shaping ways, we deserve only token positions and polite nods of recognition . . . on occasion . . . maybe if it's our birthday. If we try to step out of that assigned space, whether to make a movie or hold office or go to class, we will be reminded of our place. We will be silenced.

The evolution of the Internet—combined with our always-connected culture and the increasing demands on women in leadership to create a public following in the media—creates a perfect storm for career misogynists. Typical rules of engagement do not always apply in an online context, so it's time to get creative in our response. We can't exactly form a digital firewall around all women with a public profile. Nor is reacting to individual haters going to change anything. On the contrary, engaging those guys just gives them more ammunition, more false courage.

The Christian narrative should empower (and has empowered in the past) women to speak their truth without fear, and likewise empower men to advocate for women's voices in every frame of public life. We know that Scripture has often been used as a tool in silencing women's voices—by subverting the roles of female disciples and minimizing the voices of the relatively few women whose stories actually made it into the canon. What can people of faith now do to elevate those voices and to restore the damage done by so many years of inequality?

For one thing, we can learn to navigate technology better. That means learning to digitize ministry, engage younger generations, and better promote and communicate our message through all the wonderful avenues available to us. But it's far deeper and more complicated than that. I see lots of churches talking about how to use social media to boost worship attendance, to encourage online giving, and to build an online presence that will bring in Millennials. (Oh, the Millennials . . . we want them in church so badly, but we seem to have convinced ourselves they speak some other language.)

What I rarely hear on our social media platforms, though, is any genuine conversation about what it means to be a voice of peace, justice, and equality. Out there where the world can be so toxic and hateful, do we know how to speak a different language? Do we know how to change the narrative, how to advocate for women—especially women of color—and how to push against the patterns of misogyny that plague so many of our online interactions? It can be difficult, especially when our fluency with this world of social media varies widely across generations.

I'm on the tail end of Gen X. We identify primarily as the last generation of kids to get through high school and college unscathed by social media. Our parents, and in some cases our grandparents, have learned to use it—mostly for purposes of keeping up with *us* and our lives—and our Millennial younger siblings and our Gen Z children will never know a time without it (unless we all wind up in some dystopian tundra with no cable news and no Snapchat and no reality television, which actually doesn't sound like the worst thing). These younger generations have been largely shaped by an online narrative, while older ones have picked up the rhythms of technology in bits and pieces. Then you've got those of us hanging out in the middle—kind of a bridge between two ways of engaging the world and connecting many, many different ways of being a woman in the world.

Technology has evolved at such a breakneck pace that there have never really been any clear and ethical guidelines for rules of engagement. There definitely have been no spiritual guidelines. We've all been flying by the seat of our pants. Parents, pastors, and teachers alike wonder where to step

next—knowing full well that as soon as we figure out one element, one platform, one set of boundaries, a new app or network will explode, bringing a whole new set of challenges.

In many ways, both faith and the women's movement have
their work cut out for them. It would make all the sense in the
world for those narratives to unfold together.

For instance, people of faith—men and women alike—
should be out there on the front lines speaking out against
racism. There should be no party lines in play when a person of color is being harassed or threatened. It can be a simple
response—140 characters or less—but we who claim to follow
the way of Jesus must be the firm voice of *no* in the face of such
rhetoric. No hate, no name-calling, no overt or subtle suggestions of violence . . . not in our house, not in our church, and
not on our Facebook page. Far too often, we tend to let those
comments pass politely because we don't want drama. When
we ignore those opportunities for conversation, transformation, and genuine faith sharing, we are letting our privilege
subvert our conscience—not to mention forgetting a clear
directive of God to do justice and seek peace.

How do we bear witness when we see a woman attacked,
called names, or otherwise reduced to some element of her
appearance? Women, get other women's backs. Men, step in
more often. We need your voices more than ever to put a stop
to the shameless online bullying of the female species. This
pattern is not just about a single blustering political figure or a
single celebrity with a story to tell. This is about the systemic
silencing of literally half of the world—and half of the body of
Christ—and it is far past time we ended it, together.

Comedian Lindy West wrote a *New York Times* column
about being the guest on the podcast of some male friends.
Their series "How to Build a Better White Guy" meant to
address the layers of white male privilege inherent in their lives.
In each episode they brought on people who did not have the
kinds of privilege they enjoyed. They interviewed gay men,
people of color, women, and so on, and asked each of these

friends to help them be "better white guys," better advocates and allies. The very premise of this podcast is already a good story—and potentially a great model for faith communities that want to work for more justice in the world.

So they asked their friend Lindy, the comedian, how they could do better. And she thought about it and then she simply said, "Do you ever stick up for me?"

Well. It's a good question.

West notes the phenomenon we mentioned earlier, where the good, socially conscious guys who advocate for women tend to get laughed off the stage/off the court/out of the room. The question then becomes, *do you do what's right anyway*? Do you, as a person of faith, continue to insist on the whole personness of all? Or do you just kind of let it slide, because there's a bro code, after all, and it's just a joke? West continues:

> Our society has engineered robust consequences for squeaky wheels, a verdant pantheon from eye-rolls all the way up to physical violence. One of the subtlest and most pervasive is social ostracism—coding empathy as the fun killer, consideration for others as an embarrassing weakness and dissenting voices as out-of-touch, bleeding-heart dweebs (at best). Coolness is a fierce disciplinarian.
>
> A result is that, for the most part, the only people weathering those consequences are the ones who don't have the luxury of staying quiet. Women, already impeded and imperiled by sexism, also have to carry the social stigma of being feminist buzzkills if they call attention to it. People of color not only have to deal with racism; they also have to deal with white people labeling them "angry" or "hostile" or "difficult" for objecting.[2]

Coolness is a fierce disciplinarian. Isn't that the truth? Maybe giving up our coolness (which, let's be real, is probably imaginary) is the most powerful thing we can do right now. Our brothers and sisters in the activist community have been telling us the same thing for years about our niceness. Our commitment to being nice, to just getting along, is literally costing lives. They were right then. And they're right now.

We can't just discipline ourselves to speak up in these instances. We have to equip the body of Christ with the actual language, the talking points, the appropriate lexicon to push against the language of trolls and bullies with the language of faith. This has to do with more than just a few quotes of Scripture. It's really about empowering men to speak up for women without fear of having their masculinity called into question, and encouraging women to stand up for other women in both public and online spaces. Much like "calling in vs. calling out," there is a time and place for both real-life and digital activism in regard to women's equality. Do we have the courage to call a troll on his troll-ness, and to insist on equal respect and space for all of our sisters? To do so, we have to reject a certain myth of male dominance that inhabits all of our spaces—even the digital ones.

NO ONE IS BEYOND REDEMPTION

Furthermore—and this is critical to our children—we need to cultivate a theology of profound human worthiness—one that is not rooted in gender, race, economic class, or sexuality; one that transcends any single part of our being and taps into our inherent worth as children of God. In bringing healing to the world and equality for women, no one practice or set of words will go as far as simply teaching our children that people are people, period.

This sounds impossibly complicated, but it's really not. The notion that all people are created equal, and all are equally worthy of love and respect, is right there in Scripture. It's there at creation, when male and female are both created in the image of God. It's there in the Gospels, as Jesus reaches outside the accepted cultural norms, again and again, to draw outsiders into the fullness of life. It's even there in the early church, where people who'd had no voice before suddenly find themselves seated at the table. If we root our faith and our lives in this narrative, the way forward is clear.

When civil rights icon Ruby Sales gave her interview for *On Being*, she shared some insights about her upbringing in the black church of the South. She talks about the deep spirituality that shaped her identity in a profound way. It's that same spirituality, she says, that shaped the civil rights movement. That season of change was rooted in this deep spirit, one that empowered a whole generation for the work of great change. Relative to that upbringing, Sales sees what she calls "a crisis in white America" right now, a void of meaningful identity that leads to so much hatred of the other. She says,

> There's a spiritual crisis in white America. It's a crisis of meaning. . . . [W]e talk a lot about black theologies, but I want a liberating white theology. I want a theology that speaks to Appalachia. I want a theology that begins to deepen people's understanding about their capacity to live fully human lives and to touch the goodness inside of them rather than call upon the part of themselves that's not relational. Because there's nothing wrong with being European American. That's not the problem. It's how you actualize that history and how you actualize that reality. It's almost like white people don't believe that other white people are worthy of being redeemed.[3]

Is it possible that she's right? That we don't think each other worthy of redemption? And therefore we often refuse to engage in these difficult human issues, because we assume the troll, the bully, the white supremacist is beyond saving? We don't push back, we don't challenge the unjust assumptions, we don't even get mad anymore. We just accept that this is the way of the world. We try to stay out of the fray.

Jesus—who placed his body between a woman accused of adultery and the crowd throwing stones at her—would surely say that our silence does not fly. He'd say it is time to engage. It is time for an ethic of deep human worth that will not allow us to sit still any longer.

I do not, by any means, pretend to think that social media outlets are the best places to engage in real dialogue that will be world-shaping and life-giving. But I do know for sure that those places create a great platform for hate. So love has to show up too. Even there. Even in digital form, even from that cool distance behind the screen. Otherwise, those who silence women's voices online think they can do the same in the office, in the polls, and in the classroom. There is a time and place for all sorts of engagement here, and we are called to show up for every single one of them.

Here's the bonus to this ethic of being that reinforces the divine createdness of every person. Such a deeply human spirituality is a gift in no way tangential to the work of equality, but an equally critical piece of the puzzle. In crafting this world of worth, we teach it to our children. We teach them not only to stand up for the other and to amplify the voices of the marginalized. We teach them, in essence, to hold their own voice. We teach them, boys and girls alike, to value their own worth over and above whatever alternative messages the world and its trolling ways might sling in their direction. They will be ready in a way that their Gen X and Millennial parents had to figure out on our own. Often the hard way.

Questions for Reflection and Discussion

1. Can you think of any other ways that social media have made women more vulnerable than in previous generations? What are some ways people of faith can work to counteract those vulnerabilities?
2. How have media and technology empowered women and elevated women's voices? Can you think of examples of women's voices that we might never have heard if not for social media platforms?
3. How can we empower our churches' youth to be leaders in the frontier of justice work and social media? What

kinds of language, skills, and role models will help them in that direction?

4. When men bully and silence women online, what do you think they are missing from their own lives? What is the compassionate response?

9

Domestic Abuse and Sexual Assault: The Ongoing Tragedy

I saw a statistic once that said 83 percent of girls are sexually harassed in high school.

My first thought was, is that all?

I tell you what: 100 percent of girls are sexually harassed in high school, whether they know it or not, whether they talk about it or not. I'm pretty sure they teach a class on lewd behavior for freshmen boys. It is not a required elective, but there's a lot of peer pressure to take it.

It might seem extreme to say that all girls are harassed in high school, but think about what is meant by harassment: any touching that is unwanted; any commentary on one's body or person that feels threatening, intimidating, or demeaning; any communication that is sexual in nature, from a person with whom you are not wanting to have sexual contact.

Here's what I remember most about my ninth-grade biology class: not dissecting a frog or making a poster to label all the parts of a cell, but the harassment of a guy. Every time I walked by his desk—which was often, because of course he sat in the front row—he would call me "Body." "Hey Body." "What's up, Body?" "When are you going to sit on my lap,

Body?" That might sound harmless, but I was fifteen. When I asked why he was calling me that, he said, "Because you've got a great body." "Fine," I said, "But that's not my name." I asked him to stop, multiple times a day. He wouldn't. In fact, the more upset I got, the more he seemed to enjoy it. I ignored, I found alternate routes, I got up in his face and told him to leave me alone. But he would not quit.

I have a clear and vivid memory of slapping him clean across the face once. I'm not sure if I actually did it, or if I just day-dreamed it enough times to make it true. A good, firm, decisive whop, like the busty dames in the old movies. I can almost feel it. To this day, I don't know if I actually smacked that lascivious grin off his face, or if I just sat there seething. I'm pretty sure I sat there seething. I also started surrounding myself with male friends any time he was around. You know what? It worked. Believe me, I'm glad, always, to have good and decent men in my life (some of those, from twenty-five-plus years ago, are still friends now), but a woman should not have to create a perimeter of maleness around herself just to go walking around the world.

While I can't remember if I ever properly smacked the guy or not, I do know that I seriously hate biology, to this day. All the science things, really. You know, it all makes sense now. *It's this guy's fault I'm a minister and not a surgeon.*

Anyway, that's how I remember those instances (because there were others) from high school. I remember stomping toes, throwing elbows to ribs, and shoving boys-who-thought-they-were-men into the bright blue lockers. But I mostly just tried to walk the other way. This just seemed like a part of life I was supposed to learn to accept—and not just in high school. Women deal with this behavior from grown-ass men, every day—often in situations where the man is an authority figure of some kind. But it all starts right here: on the bus, in the locker room, behind the bleachers. It starts in boys getting a thousand little messages a day that women's bodies exist for their amusement, pleasure, and use, and girls getting a thou-sand little messages a day that they are powerless against the force of masculine entitlement.

Hey, it's a compliment.

Geez, relax.

You're such a prude.

High school girls—even junior high girls—are in a fish bowl. No, a zoo. Boys act this way, and you can't exactly up and leave. You are at school. You are a captive audience for the theater of male adolescence and its often unchecked exuberance. Teachers, parents, counselors, youth ministers, and coaches all need to be aware of these gender dynamics and take an active role in reprogramming boys to see their female peers as more than objects. Coaches especially have power to help boys channel that energy for good and not for evil, to shift the expectations of how they engage the opposite sex from something that smacks of "boys will be boys" to something that looks like respectful and dignified interaction. Isn't this the precise place where locker-room talk begins, the first place it's accepted to refer to a female classmate as some territory to be conquered and not as an actual person? Adults who are present and engaged can nip that in the bud, if they are paying attention.

Of course, respect for women must be modeled first at home, or nothing that happens at church, school, or practice is going to have a lasting impact. But we'd be surprised at the potential positive effects of peer pressure in groups of boys. If more boys than not were likely to say, "Hey, she's my friend," or "Don't talk about her like that," that wouldn't necessarily stop the behavior entirely. But it would begin to break down the message that this is the norm, that it's socially acceptable to treat and speak about women as though they are not quite human people but bodies to be judged, acquired, and dominated.

In school settings, any coverage of this topic is often reactive. It doesn't come up until it's already a problem—at which time the administrators may or may not have effective ways of addressing the behavior. Even then, the response is focused purely on the matter of harassment, not on the deeper issue of subverting women. Instead of reacting when boys act out, we need to be proactive at young ages, in modeling boundaries and respect for boys and empowerment for girls.

We didn't have words for it exactly when I was younger—or if we did, no adult ever taught them to us—but now we do. My highly common experience in freshman biology is called rape culture. Not that all boys who grab asses are going to be rapists. But I guarantee you that most rapists started out as ass-grabbers, catcallers, and leering idiots in biology class. The technical description of rape culture is a society or environment whose prevailing social attitudes have the effect of normalizing or trivializing sexual assault and abuse.

Pretty much every high school you know, right? Not to mention that much of what we see on television, and much of the messaging that advertisers use to make us want things, contributes to this culture as well, saturating the broader culture in which we live.

As a teenager, I was highly involved in youth group. I was at church every time the doors opened. I had good friends there and healthy relationships with both men and women. As I mentioned before, it was a progressive-ish church, where no one gave me the notion that I was an inferior or secondary species because of my gender. Yet *nothing* in my church upbringing equipped me to stand up for myself. Nothing in my lexicon of faith prepared me to push back against those early lessons in male aggression. I'm sure people were talking about things like rape culture, consent, and widespread objectification back then, but it wasn't part of the mainstream discourse—certainly not in southeastern Kentucky.

In the decades since, as psychology and social science have evolved, so too has the ability of the faith community to engage in dialogue about this topic. Youth curricula like "Created by God," "Our Whole Lives," and "Eighters Camp" (a summer church camp curriculum specifically designed for eighth graders) are now utilized in many churches to teach kids/youth about body image and sexuality, emphasizing healthy boundaries and healthy attitudes toward sexuality, body image, and bodily autonomy. It is critical that churches and families employ these resources right now because rape culture is so entrenched in kids from a young age. The acceptance of harassment inherent in our mainstream culture cannot be separated from the kinds of aggression that take on physical form. Granted, my experience with adolescent verbal harassment was not nearly as traumatic as a sexual assault. But the culture that condones one condones the other, and both need to be addressed as two symptoms of the same illness: a misogynous worldview in which women's bodies are not really their own.

SANITIZING THE HEADLINES

Such a heartbreaking story, they said. Such a gifted young man, with a promising future, they sighed. Sadly, he was brought down by a loose woman who drank too much and didn't know how to keep herself from getting raped while she was unconscious. It's a shame.

That was the gist of the *Washington Post* article about Brock Turner, in the wake of his sexual assault on a woman attending a fraternity party at Stanford University, where Turner was a freshman. It was pretty much a dead giveaway that this was going to be a "sympathy for the devil" piece when the headline led with "All-American Swimmer Brock Turner." There are many other things they could have said in that headline. How about "another privileged white boy who had every opportunity to *not* commit a violent crime"? Or "affluent kid who has grown up feeling entitled to everything, apparently including women's bodies"? But they led with his star-athlete status, including, at some point in the piece, his best breaststroke time. This became a story about all that had been lost—*for him*. Adding to that narrative, Turner's *father* penned a letter to the judge, outlining all the reasons that his son should not be punished for "twenty minutes of action." That was the part, I think, that caused the letter to go viral. Women everywhere (and more than a few good men) had a visceral reaction to hearing sexual violence dismissed in such a grotesque way.

Rape is a violent, heinous crime and should be punished to
the full extent of the law. Every time. No matter how white,
privileged, and otherwise "promising" the perpetrator. This
was shameful reporting, but it also reflects an important truth
about rape culture: storytelling matters. The way the media
completely sanitized his image for the story contributes to the
overall normalizing of assault.

Instead, the outlet should have shared the account of the
young woman he victimized. She publicly and powerfully
shared how her own "promising future" had been affected by
this crime. But they didn't tell her story. Instead, they shared
her rapist's swimming times and a great picture for his online
dating profile, glossing over his violent actions with an air of
"Don't worry, son; you'll get your life back." This kind of
journalism contributes, in big ways, to the culture in which
a woman's body is never going to be as important as "the all-
American athlete/scholar/hero" who was brought down by his
proximity to her.

In cases like this one, which are all too common, the media
profile colors not only the way in which the general public will
view the incident, but possibly even how the judge will view
the defendant—even if the defendant is found guilty by the
jury of his peers. With the judicial system at their sides, even
convicted rapists often get by with just a few months in prison
(as with Brock Turner), sometimes just a few weeks. When a
forty-nine-year-old teacher in Montana was charged with rap-
ing a fourteen-year-old student, the judge gave him thirty days,
saying that the girl was "equally in charge" of what was going
on.[1] That girl later killed herself, indicating to anyone with
eyes to see that she felt in no way in charge.

We know that rape is not about sex but about power, about
the right that men feel to exert force over a woman's body,
because the culture at large has condoned that sense of entitlement. Clearly, that sense of a woman's body not being her own
extends far beyond the perpetrator and deep into our legal system. Judges who hand down a symbolic jail sentence with a
wink and a nod are just the tip of the iceberg. We hear horror

stories of police, taking accounts of assault survivors and asking, "Well, what were you doing there?" or "Why on earth were you walking alone at night?" This is a common line of questioning, from law enforcement as well as friends, family, and reporters. Most states in America have a backlog of rape kits—an estimated 175,000 nationwide[2]—taken in area hospitals and turned over to law enforcement but never processed. In many cases, it's because the city lacks the personnel and the resources to shoulder the expense. But the bottom line is that few convictions ever come of the testing; it's just really not a priority.

The systems that enforce and uphold the law are a big part of the problem, but so are lawmakers themselves. Our legislators prove, again and again, that they do not value women's bodies when they vote against measures that would protect women. People in power often lack basic understanding of what sexual assault even is, or how a woman's body works. In a 2016 interview about the right to terminate pregnancies that occur as a result of rape, Representative Todd Akin said that a woman's body has "ways of shutting that whole thing down" in cases of "legitimate rape."[3] If it was *really* rape (which the word "legitimate" indicates that Akin believes is a rare and often exaggerated occurrence), a woman's body just magically knows how to not get pregnant. While that kind of ignorance is now jarring to hear, it used to be a pretty commonly held belief that a woman gets pregnant only if she enjoyed the sex or "asked for it"; therefore, there is no such thing as pregnancy from rape.[4] While we may view that as an ancient worldview, it clearly has some holdovers alive and well and living among us.

It's just a pity that those holdovers happen to make their way into elected office.

When our government, legal system, and culture at large devalue women at every turn, it's no wonder that one in five women will be sexually assaulted in her lifetime. It's no wonder that only about five out of every *thousand* perpetrators of sexual violence will suffer legal consequences.[5]

The world watched Steubenville, Ohio, as a trial unfolded in the gang rape of a girl. On trial was basically the whole high school football team. In this trial one of the defendants said of the victim that she was seen as "community property," even though she'd been seeing one of his teammates.[6] *Community property.* That's actually a pretty astute understanding of how the world views women's bodies. Girls and women themselves internalize that message in alarming ways, and often instances of assault and abuse go unreported. Why bother, victims think, when their assailants will go unpunished? Boys' entitlement to women's bodies is, in a very real sense, the unofficial law of the land.

This is a sickness. It's not a new sickness, by any stretch. But it's a sickness that has found new expression in the age of social media and as women have gained more power in other spheres of public life. As women gain traction in leadership, rights, and public autonomy, it's no wonder that sexual assault statistics pretty much stay at the same alarmingly high rates. When women find voice in public life, the patriarchy finds other ways to subdue and silence them.

Of course, sexual violence is not the only kind of violence that women endure. In the United States, a woman is assaulted or beaten every nine seconds. One in three have been abused physically by a domestic partner. One in seven women has had a stalker. Domestic violence hotlines in this country receive about 20,800 calls a day.[7] These numbers never cease to startle us, but they don't seem to change much from year to year. That's because, however many public-health campaigns we wage on violence against women—and violence has been declared a public-health crisis—little will change as long as we fail to address the underlying cultural messages that lead to such treatment of women and their bodies.

ENDING THE CYCLE

Like the cycles of poverty, the cycles of abuse should serve as a profound calling for the church to get involved in the work of women's equality. When the church defers on this matter—perhaps supporting the local domestic-abuse shelter but not engaging the deeper, systemic issues of violence against women—it essentially disregards its own complicity in the structures that enable such violence. It also misses out on the biblical imperative to seek justice for the isolated, the abused, and those disempowered by imbalanced systems. As with work to interrupt cycles of poverty, there are ways that the church— often uniquely situated to organize and advocate on behalf of those with little voice—can engage local and state government, without violating boundaries of church and state.

For example, the Supreme Court recently ruled that prior domestic-violence offenders not be allowed to purchase firearms. While this should seem like a no-brainer, it was actually a heated partisan debate. Even now, that ruling is not widely enforced. It would not be an overtly political move for the church to engage local law enforcement and find out what protections are in place for women who have been victims of domestic violence, or what procedures are followed when prosecuting an instance of sexual assault. Is your local municipality processing rape kits, for instance? Are women consistently notified when their attackers are released from jail? Simple matters like this make all the difference in those alarming statistics. If the community of faith lent its voice to local accountability, it would go a long way to change the lives of women.

But perhaps the most powerful thing the church can do to shift the culture in this regard is simply to stop teaching complementarianism, the belief that men and women each have different God-ordained gifts and purposes. Whether this view is rooted in a misreading of Scripture or just the cultural biases that have plagued faith from the beginning, many faith leaders still embrace it. On the surface, that doesn't sound like a harmful worldview, but the whole "different but equal" narrative falls apart when you delve into the notion of a man's intended "headship." The woman is intended to "complement" the man's authority—ultimately by upholding his word, serving his needs, and taking on otherwise supportive roles.

When held as a set of personal beliefs, perhaps this understanding works in a few families who are uniquely suited, within appropriate boundaries, to live out this dynamic. But by and large, this kind of gender role designation contributes to and perpetuates the toxic cycles of abuse against women. That sneaky notion of man as authoritative, buried within the fabric of the church itself, helps perpetuate the notion that women's bodies are not entirely our own, that women who resist their designated role or posture need to be subdued and silenced. Complementarianism, and other theological nods to patriarchy, carry the subtle message that a woman's body is merely for the pleasure of a man or to be dominated at will.

Until we stop telling girls that God made them second, to be secondary, we will continue to teach boys that the world is theirs for the taking.

Barring a complete overnight upheaval of our societal and theological structures, perhaps there are other faithful ways to equip our boys and our girls to establish healthy boundaries, meaningful relationships, and an ethic of human worth that will push against the trends of violence against women. These are important—even critical—conversations to have, both at home and in the faith community, as children age. With time and intention, we can begin to shift the dynamics that lead to widespread and systemic abuse of women's bodies.

> —*Create a climate of trust, not control.* Which would you rather your teenage daughter say to her new boyfriend: (a) "I can't wait for you to meet my parents" or (b) "I'm going to have to sneak out to meet you at that party because my dad will kill you and my mom will kill me"? You do the math. Cultivating open dialogue about our bodies and sexuality will mean youth and young adults who are more comfortable in their own skin, and more equipped to process relationships within the framework of the family system. It also creates the expectation that parents need to spend time with anyone their child is spending time with.

— *Teach boundaries and consent.* It is OK to refuse a hug. No means no. Repeat. Experts say never to force a child to hug or kiss someone when they don't want to. Having ownership of our bodies is not rudeness. It is personal space. This seems like a simple thing, but it goes a long way to teach both boys and girls that their body is their own.

— *Talk about hard things.* Sex, death, math homework, bullies, you name it. If you can get comfortable talking about that which is scary or confounding to your kids, then they will get comfortable with you as a source of comfort and information.

— *Take the shame out of sex.* There is nothing wrong or sinful about desire. Our bodies are not an enemy or a liability, but part of God's good creation. Everyone, regardless of their gender, is responsible for making healthy, informed decisions *for themselves.* Meanwhile, you do hope for your children to have a healthy sex life at an age-appropriate time in his or her life. Removing a sense of shame from sexual desire will make girls feel more empowered to resist unwanted sexual advances and make boys less likely to develop dominating behavior.

— *Emphasize self-worth.* Model it, build it, nurture it. In a thousand little ways, we can remind our kids that they are more than their successes and failures; that they are worthy, loved by us and God, no matter what; and that *anybody who doesn't treat them well does not deserve to be around them.* A healthy sense of self is one of the most powerful tools we can give our kids.

While these specific practices can go a long way to shift a culture of male dominance and sexual violence, perhaps the best gift the church can offer the world is to raise children and youth to view all of their neighbors as fully human, embodied children of God—not objects, not lesser beings, not broken, sinful, or shameful bodies, but fully human, created in the image of the divine.

Ultimately, the culture of dominating women is complex. It takes many forms: verbal harassment, sexual assault, domestic abuse, and the thousand little messages a day that our bodies are not quite our own. The cycles of abuse are multilayered, as are the systems that uphold them. So the response must be multilayered, as well. We need the voices of lawmakers, law enforcement, parents, teachers, *and* faith leaders to fully address the ongoing war on women. Furthermore, the approaches need to be both practical and philosophical, legislative and theological. No one organization can undo a system that affects every part of our culture; but if we can engage all of these systems together, we can more effectively dismantle the myth that women's bodies are community property.

My friend C. Shawn McGuffey is a professor at Boston College, a scholar, a historian, and an expert in gender, race, sexuality, and trauma. He has worked extensively with sexual assault survivors. He recently shared with me a word that should be shared far and wide with people of faith who want to curb the trends of violence against women:

> I've helped organize four different sexual assault coping programs for women in four different churches in four different cities. One thing that sticks out to me that came up over and over again is that many women felt that the Church and scripture encouraged violence against women; whether through teachings that women should be submissive to men, that divorce is against God, or that women might need to endure violence to maintain a marriage.
>
> With this in mind I would suggest explicitly teaching theology that speaks against violence against women. All four programs at all four churches requested that their pastors and church leadership explicitly address these issues in sermons and Bible studies. They also requested that this be put in Church charter and distributed. All said this was helpful for their recovery. Also, although men were not the focus of the groups, many men came up to me and said this was also helpful because it gave them a way to discuss these issues with other men.[8]

Providing safe spaces for this kind of dialogue would be a faithful way forward for a church of any tradition or ideology. The trends of violence against women are not a divisive political matter or a "woman's issue," but a call to God's people everywhere to resist rape culture and the norms of domination that too often begin and end in the Christian narrative.

Questions for Reflection and Discussion

1. Think about commercials, radio ads, music, billboards, and other messaging that you have seen today. Have you spotted any underlying implications that women are weak? Or that men are strong? What about glorified violence? How do these messages influence a culture that condones (or politely ignores) violence against women?
2. What are some ways that the Christian narrative perpetuates the cycle of abuse against women? How can we work to undo those teachings?
3. Who in your community is doing good work to empower women and prevent violence? How could you and/or your church contribute to the work they are doing?

10

The Political Uterus and Hope of a Better Way

Mrs. Harding had tried everything else. Chugging gin. A scalding hot bath. Hitting herself forcefully in the stomach. Taking Epsom salts. When none of that worked, the desperate mother of eight paid the neighborhood "healer," Mrs. Pritchard, to do what she'd done for countless others in the community. She brought out her rubber sheet and her rusty tools. Then ensued one of the hardest-to-watch episodes of television to ever come forth from the usually docile PBS, as season two, episode five of *Call the Midwife* delved into a painful, terrifying, and deeply controversial story line about abortion.[1]

Mrs. Harding wound up suffering from septicemia, falling into a coma, and struggling near to death with the fallout. By the end of the episode she had made a full recovery. The same could not be said of the viewing audience. The show's creators and producers endured fierce and immediate fallout from viewers who felt the topic—and the graphic manner in which it was portrayed—was too intense and disturbing for television. But the truth is that the horrors of an unsafe and illegal abortion, in both the UK and the United States, are specters of

a not-too-distant past. For women around the world, they are
an all-too-present reality, even today.

For all the controversy of that episode, the series *Call the
Midwife* explores the lives of women, and the world of wom-
en's health, in a way far more compassionate and nuanced than
we seem capable of doing in our own day, in real life.

We know that the best way to keep a disenfranchised group
on the margins is to divide them from within the ranks. Keep
persons at odds with others who share their social status, and
that marginalized group as a whole will never find the momen-
tum to rally and fight for their own freedom. Find a wedge
issue that will take their eyes off who the real oppressor is—
something highly contentious and emotional, something that
will ensure a raging battle that will evolve over generations—
and the group will completely forget its objectionable status
and keep fighting within itself.

In many ways, abortion is *the* most effective wedge issue
possible, because it draws in so many of the other matters of
inequality that keep women marginalized. The conversation
about women's health and reproductive rights—when properly nuanced—touches on the issues of poverty, sexual assault,
rape culture, the wage gap, access to affordable health care, and
a woman's right to exercise autonomy over her own body. Yet
the dialogue often bypasses these more complex issues entirely,
establishing black-and-white, right-and-wrong boundaries and
demonizing women who wander into the surrounding gray
areas of uncertainty or even a little bit of discernment. Religious and political leaders alike have learned how to effectively
divide and conquer women by rejecting the nuance and going
straight for the shame.

Whatever our feelings on the matter of abortion, we should
all cringe when white men sign a bill that will affect women
worldwide—and then use that photo opportunity as the center
of their reelection strategy. We could have a much healthier,
more nuanced, and more compassionate discussion about this
if we took the men—and the rhetoric and the ideology—out of
the picture. What might that look like in practice? How can we

keep this conversation from getting hijacked, again and again, by extreme ideologies on both ends of the spectrum?

Women have tremendous gifts for solving problems, making connections, and finding creative ways to approach seemingly insurmountable issues. The other thing we know? Church ladies run the world. Seriously. The church ladies I know can feed an army on a moment's notice; run the community food drive/charity walk/chili cook-off fundraiser while blindfolded; make sure every kid in town has a toy for Christmas; and/or pull together an Easter pageant while juggling the details of the egg hunt and fixing the roof. Again. They can do all that with a smile (because they are genuinely happy to serve and want to smile, not because some man *told us to smile*) and a good hair day. So shouldn't women of faith be able to tackle the complex matter of women's reproductive health, together, in a loving and constructive way? If we could for just a moment lay aside the ideology and the party-line sound bites, drawing instead on our own God-given strengths and the gospel message of grace and compassion, I am certain we could find a way out of this stalemate.

NO EASY ANSWERS

I classify myself as personally pro-life and politically pro-choice. While that sounds hypocritical to some, it is in fact a critical nuance that people of faith need to consider if we are ever going to move this conversation forward, out of the realm of wedge-issue politics. While it has been a cash chip leveraged by politicians for many years now, it is in fact a deeply human issue, with many human angles that cannot be reduced to a cheap sound bite for cable news. A philosophy that is truly for life must reach far beyond the womb.

Like many, many women (and men) I know, I am a Christian who believes in the sanctity of life. I am deeply unsettled by the number of pregnancies that are terminated in America every year. Any loss of life is tragic. However, I recognize that my opinion

on this matter comes from a place of privilege. I've never lived
in poverty or worried how I would feed myself—much less my
child. I've never been raped or physically abused. I have always
had access to health care. Therefore, while I am against abortion,
I don't feel entitled to make that decision for every woman.

The more I learn about life in countries where abortion is
not legal, the more certain I am that reproductive choice is critical to civilized society. I once read a chilling profile about the
women of El Salvador, where reproductive rights are severely
limited—as is access to birth control. In fact, that nation has
one of the most restrictive sets of laws in the world when it
comes to women's health. In such a country, many women
wind up in *prison* for having miscarriages—not abortions in a
clinic, but *naturally occurring miscarriages*. If women in El Salvador (and other places like it) can't "prove" that it was unin-
tentional (and no one is really sure how they might prove such
a thing), they can face criminal charges.[2]

Imagine, for the moment, the trauma of going through a
miscarriage—which about one-quarter of women will experience at some point—and then having to bear the burden of
proof that you did not *intentionally* end the pregnancy. There
is no proving it. So a (probably male) judge decides whether
he trusts your face, whether you look as if you may be a slut,
whether you are dressed appropriately, whether you have the
right family references or job, whether you fit his arbitrary
description of a properly grieving mother. So on top of the
horrific physical and emotional experience you've just endured,
you are faced with the possibility of imprisonment—up to
thirty years—for the "crime."

If you researched life in any country that places such restrictions on women—or, better yet, got to know some of those
women—you would never, for a moment, consider it a country that values the sanctity of life. You would come away knowing it is a country that is hostile to women, that wants only to
control, manipulate, and silence half of its population. If you
want to refute *that* fact, find out how many men in those countries are prosecuted for their role in said unwanted pregnancy.

It's easy to say, "That would never happen in America." But—make no mistake—laws that limit access to abortion are laws that limit care for women, in general. And the unintended consequences inherent in some of those laws—which are drafted, by and large, by men—would be unforeseeable, on the whole, in our relatively civilized culture. There may be allowances for victims of rape or incest to terminate a pregnancy, but that is a dangerously small loophole. In those cases, the burden of proof would fall on the victim; which could tie up the process in all kinds of red tape and drama, which would push the procedure into a late-term termination.

The idea of more (or any) late-term abortions—contrary to most conservative rhetoric to the contrary—is a disturbing prospect for even the most pro-choice among us. Meanwhile, most folks who classify themselves as exclusively pro-life, in the most political of terms, do not realize that this is the world they are asking us to inhabit, a world where a woman can go to jail for a terrible loss that is an act of nature. It's the world women in many developing countries must endure every day. We like to think we are more civilized than that. It turns out, maybe we are not.

Just ask the doctors who serve the poorest, most vulnerable, and least educated women in our own country—those women who stand as conviction of our own comfort and privilege, in many cases, for the ways they were left out of the comforts and assumptions of middle-class life. Those doctors here would tell you the same thing: abortion is a heart-breaking reality, but access is necessary to civilization and to the whole-personness of womanhood.

A doctor I know did part of her medical training in the Atlanta metro area. As a young ob-gyn, she volunteered one day a week at a clinic that provided abortions. She was always on her guard walking into that place (and even now we are keeping her identity private), knowing there could be protestors, maybe some prone to violence. But she did it anyway, believing it to be a part of the job, part of the calling. Of course, other parts of the job are important too. Like providing access to birth control, *especially* for underprivileged women following multiple pregnancies.

Dr. A, we will call her, says that about half of all pregnancies in the United States are unplanned. And while some of those unplanned pregnancies will be carried to term, ultimately about one in three American women will have an abortion in her lifetime. I find that statistic staggering—and heartbreaking. But it just goes to show, this is not the issue of a certain class, race, age group, or even belief system of women. It is literally "Every Third Woman"[3] in this country. If we want to see any sort of turn in those numbers, we have to change the conversation.

I value Dr. A's insight, and I think strong, educated women like her could really pave the way for a more productive dialogue. As a person of faith, she considers herself to be pro-life. "I deliver babies," she said. "It's the best part of the job. What could be more pro-life than that?" Yet she recognizes that if abortions are not legal, they will not be safe. Countless women will seek the procedure anyway and will be at risk for septic abortion—a problem that has all but disappeared in the developed world with the legalization of abortion. Her professional and also faith-based insight is this: "In order to be truly pro-life, as a society you also have to be pro-legal abortion." That doesn't mean that you encourage or celebrate abortion but that, as a civilized nation, you keep access legal and the procedure safe—and meanwhile pour resources into preventative care, education, and advocacy for women.

One of the most shocking things I learned from our conversation is that in many states doctors are required by law to read a script to patients seeking abortion—a government-prescribed script that contains false information, including a link between abortion and breast cancer.[4] There is no scientific evidence of such a correlation. Yet these are things that our (male) legislators think women need to be told. By their doctors. In 2017.

If that isn't about shame and control, then I don't know what it is.

It is worth noting that the countries with the most restrictive abortion laws do *not*, in fact, have lower rates of abortion.[5] What they do have is high rates of desperate women who obtain illegal and dangerous abortions. Large numbers of "doctors" who are really butchers, perfectly willing to take a vulnerable woman's money and leave her for dead. Women who are poor, vulnerable, and victims of life in extremely patriarchal systems and worldviews. Women who perhaps got pregnant without their consent and are now legally bound to carry the pregnancy to term. Women who could not possibly care for and feed an infant while keeping their jobs—in many cases, making low-cost goods for us to buy in our suburban American department stores. Women who may be kicked out of their family's home for the shame of a pregnancy under any number of circumstances. The list goes on and on. But the bottom line is, the typical middle-class American Christian enjoys a set of privileges that makes it almost impossible to comprehend the real-life circumstances of many of the world's women—circumstances that make abortion access not just a necessity, but a mercy. If we do not want life for women in our country to digress in similar fashion, then we have to extend the same access, the same mercy to the women here at home, and to trust those women to make the right decision for their own bodies, their own families.

It is complicated and heartbreaking and complicated some more. But we cannot possibly be so arrogant as to think we can make a decision about that woman's body or baby.

ROOT CAUSES, NOT RHETORIC

There are ways that we can, within the parameters of a free and developed civilization, dramatically reduce the number of abortions, ways forward for the contemporary church to engage this work in a way that is life-giving, faithful, and deeply transformative. Rather than controlling and punishing women, we can examine and seek to alleviate the factors that cause women to seek abortions in the first place.

For one thing, we can address systemic poverty, the kind of abject need that makes it difficult for a woman to care for a child. The lingering wage gap, discussed in chapter 6, is one of the primary contributing factors to the cycles of poverty, especially among women and children. If people of faith could effectively curb the trends that keep women in poverty, lacking in education and opportunity for generations on end, then we could make huge strides in empowering women to make informed and intentional decisions about their procreative health. At the same time, if we could effectively provide access to preventative and contraceptive health services, the number of unwanted pregnancies would drop dramatically. Not to mention, if women knew they would have at least basic health care covered for their child, they might be more willing to become mothers; and this would also remove the intimidating cost factor of a hospital delivery. Teen pregnancy in America is actually at an *all-time low* right now, thanks in large part to the Affordable Care Act and easier access to birth control and sex education.

We can also address the epidemic of sexual and domestic violence against women, and the obvious implications of male dominance for women's health and well-being overall. Clearly, when women (including married women) are raped or coerced to have sex by threat of violence, this can result in unwanted pregnancies. Abusive relationships can also make women reluctant to bring a child into the home. Again, urging our lawmakers to pursue legislation that would actually result in prosecution for perpetrators and greater protections for women is a good start. We can also, at the local level, support domestic-violence shelters in our communities. Do some homework though. Learn which programs are offering a band-aid of temporary shelter, and which ones are actually working for prevention and culture change. If there's not such a program in your community, what a powerful ministry that would be for some local congregation to undertake as a part of their own mission!

These actionable steps get ignored when we succumb to polarizing rhetoric that declines to consider the root causes of the issue we're debating. It seems like a no-brainer that fewer unwanted pregnancies means fewer abortions; but many politicians refuse to draw (or acknowledge) that line of logic, opting instead to capitalize on the deeply emotional fervor of the religious right. Christians must become immune to meaningless lip service . . . because anyone can say they care about life.

Consider how suddenly, only four months prior to election day, Donald Trump experienced a supposed religious conversion and was subsequently super concerned with all the unborn babies.[6] It was a grotesque display of pandering but sadly was not a unique display in the world of politics. Just take a look at any male politician who has ever leveraged the pro-life vote to put him over the edge in a close election, or any man, on either side of the aisle, who has ever manipulated the single-issue voter demographic for his own political gain (whatever that one issue might be). The list of such political leaders is as long as the line of protestors outside the abortion clinic. After all, when a large swath of the voting population openly acknowledges that abortion is *the* issue that determines their ballot pick, then it is easy for an opportunistic politician (again, likely a man) to manipulate that field. The single-issue ballot mentality is truly an open invitation for the most corrupt, disingenuous, and opportunistic among us to rise to the top of the political sphere.

The end result is a toxic dialogue rooted in sound bites, out-of-context Scripture, and shame that doesn't really value life at all, but instead capitalizes on all of our deepest fears and biases about women and the inherent liability of women's bodies. In fact, many of those who stake their campaigns on a pro-life platform are the very political leaders who are openly hostile toward women. To think that these men will advocate for policies that value life, let alone its sanctity, is absurd. Yet the rampant success of such candidates among evangelical and conservative mainline Christians just goes to show how much power such a stump speech can yield.

Meanwhile, many Christians counted it as a loss when the Supreme Court overturned a Texas abortion ban in 2016.[7] The ban was one of many measures employed nationwide to limit women's access to providers that offered abortion services. While keeping abortion legal (per *Roe v. Wade*), such measures impose restrictions on the providers and facilities themselves, making providing abortions so costly or personnel-prohibitive that the facilities ultimately close. The fine print, though, is that such bans limit women's access to other kinds of care as well. So overturning the ban was a vote for women's rights, which, in turn, was a vote for children, including unborn ones.

On the same day, the U.S. Supreme Court upheld a law to ban domestic-violence perpetrators from buying guns (how was this even still a question?), which was another vote for women. Measures like these do far more to reduce abortion rates in the long run than any restrictive measure that tries to limit women's access to care. Supreme Court judges, ideally free from the impulses of political pandering, have done some good things that address the actual life factors that might lead a woman to seek an abortion. While those holding a certain ideology about the matter would count such progress as a loss, these measures are good for women, all around.

Good news for women is good news for everyone.

Productive conversations about abortion cannot take place on a political debate stage, or at a rally where emotions are high and people are shouting obscenities and waving posters of dismembered babies, or in the comments section of an online opinion piece. But I can sit down at a table with my friend Valerie—whose sociopolitical and religious views are wildly divergent from mine, in every way—and we can engage in a sane, compassionate, and actually productive conversation about this matter . . . because we are sane, compassionate, civic-minded people. When the chips are down, we may wind up voting differently. That's because the people who frame this dialogue for the political stage *need* for us to be at odds with each other. It benefits them politically (and maybe even financially). But if Valerie and I ran the world, I am confident that we could find a way forward that values the life of the unborn while also holding concern for women who find themselves in painful, sometimes even impossible, situations.

At the heart, it's a matter of changing the conversation and *claiming space for women, and women's bodies, in public discourse*. As Christians, we don't get to be single-issue voters. We don't get to be single-issue *anything*. As people who follow the way of Christ, we are called to be stewards of all life: an inclusive, expansive vision of the kingdom of heaven, brought to life in real time here and now. We can't do that if our focus rests solely on what happens before birth. Nor are we faithful to that vision when the whole system in which we live is distinctly organized to control, silence, and manipulate half the population. It's time to develop, not a pro-life rhetoric or a party-line voting issue, but a *pro-life ethic*, one that encompasses stewardship of the earth, care of the poor (especially children in poverty), and the equality of all those who have been silenced by an oppressive system for too many generations to count.

A NEW DAY, A NEW WAY?

Millennial women have often felt left out of the feminist movement—because it seems like their mothers' (or grandmothers'!) fight, or because they find the conversation too divisive and unproductive, or maybe just because those on the front lines have not found a way to engage younger generations. But that doesn't mean younger women are not finding new and innovative ways of approaching women's issues, women's equality, and women's health.

A feature in *Marie Claire*, a magazine primarily for young women, explores a growing movement of "feminist atheist pro-life Millennials." If that sounds like a big bag of paradoxes, this feminist Christian pro-choice-ish Gen Xer is right there with you. But read on. It's fascinating. Many of these young women identify as the

> secular anti-abortion movement, a small but growing group of mostly young adults who place abortion in the realm of human rights, not theology. And while 61% of American Millennials believe abortion should be legal, young secular pro-lifers are gaining steam in communities online and around the country. . . . By speaking in terms of biology instead of theology, secular abortion opponents separate themselves from their religious counterparts— the group that has dominated the movement thus far. They also seek to pull away from pro-life's more extremist, reactionary, and "exploitive of the unborn" factions, which are a turn-off for many Millennials who traffic in sentiments like "Love is Love is Love." When her group passed a truck papered with photographs of the body parts of fetuses with the words "murder" on it and a photo of Planned Parenthood President Cecile Richards with blood photoshopped onto her hands, (movement leader) Murphy muttered under her breath, "Ugh, why am I pro-life again?"[8]

Well . . . in many ways they are pro-life because the belief in the sanctity of that life runs deep . . . deeper than any theology or ideology or movement can claim as its own exclusive territory. But this wave of young women is pro-life in a different way. For instance, they are less focused on the legal end of the discussion—criminalizing abortion and restricting access—and more focused on a conversation that will transform people's views on the matter. "If you overturn *Roe v. Wade* and make abortion illegal, we're still going to be having abortions," says Rosemary Geraghty, one of the emerging leaders of the movement, "at least until society becomes pro-life*time*, not just pro-life." For this reason she intentionally focuses her activism on cultural change. "I support equal legal protections for all human beings, but I think overturning *Roe* *v. Wade* could lead to unsafe abortions if our country doesn't respect pre-born life."[9]

While this new expression of the women's movement (if they would even call themselves that) is far from perfect or complete, it rightly puts the emphasis not on a pro-life vote but on a *pro-life ethic,* which is far more encompassing than a single social or ideological issue. While their movement is distinctly secular, those in the faith-based work of equality can certainly learn a great deal from these younger women about nuance, holding space for complexity, and making room at the table for people with widely divergent beliefs and backgrounds.

If a secular movement can take a fresh approach at this nuance, if a television show like *Call the Midwife* can tell an engaging and convicting story of life and hope and privilege, then how much more equipped should God's people be to engage this conversation in a new and life-giving way. We have the language of the gospel and stories of resurrection to share; we have the call to care for all creation, the call to live in community, the directive to love neighbor as self and to approach the world with empathy: all as part of the narrative of faith. With these truths so deeply engrained in our collective being, surely we can answer the call to sit in the tension that surrounds this deeply fractious issue and speak instead to the real human life at the center.

In addition to the gospel itself, there are other resources available to help navigate this matter faithfully. One of the most in-depth and helpful that I've found is Kira Schlesinger's *Pro-Choice and Christian: Reconciling Faith, Politics, and Justice.* This is a great conversation starter for faith groups or even families that want to move beyond the rhetoric and dig a little deeper into relevant Scripture and work toward a broader understanding of what it means to be in favor of life.

The Religious Coalition for Reproductive Choice also serves as a great resource for engaging faithful dialogue about reproductive health and justice. They address everything from access to affordability of services and provide a wide range of interfaith materials to help guide productive discussion.[10]

While a certain brand of conservative Christians has developed a reputation for being dogmatic and extreme in its pro-life stance, in truth most American Christians place themselves in some nebulous in-between when it comes to their belief. Yet many communities of faith shy away from real conversation about the tensions and complexity most of us know is there, crying, "Too divisive!" "Too controversial!" and, of course, "Too political!" Perhaps that is true. A church, of course, should not align itself with a party or politician (although many do so anyway). But when we relegate the matter to just the framework of politics, many human factors get overlooked. And matters of abortion, women's health care, and the well-being of children are certainly human factors.

The church has allowed politicians to hijack and monopolize the debate for their own personal gain, because that's what the patriarchy does. It dominates and manipulates and ultimately wants to subvert and subdue. What if the church were to take back some critical pieces of this dialogue? It would not be a matter of the church getting political but, rather, of people of faith having a faithful conversation about a human issue that's become way too political. If the church wants to be truly countercultural—and believers in both conservative and progressive Christian circles claim that as a goal—what could be more transformative than reclaiming a faithful voice at the heart of this conversation, coming out of our respective corners, and approaching with practical solutions that are truly life-giving for all?

At the heart of the call to develop a truly pro-life ethic lies a deeply embodied understanding of women and men as fully and finally equal. A theology of worthiness, when processed through the local congregation and the wider body of believers, will touch every part of public and private life as we know it. It holds the power to deeply transform the world.

Questions for Reflection and Discussion

1. What do you see as the biggest barrier to engaging a compassionate and more nuanced discussion about reproductive rights?
2. Name some of the philosophies and practices at the heart of an all-encompassing pro-life ethic. What issues besides abortion does this ethic address?
3. How might learning about women's lives in other parts of the world help us better approach this matter? How does the matter of "life" relate to the broader themes of equality for women?
4. How can the community of faith shift the focus of this topic from the political sphere to a spiritual one?

Conclusion

As I put the finishing touches on this manuscript, I was called to the hospital. One of our youth had gotten seriously ill at school and was rushed to the ER.

It was a beautiful early fall day in the Midwest as I pulled into one of four clergy parking spots. (*Four!* A clergy parking spot, if you don't know it, is pure gold. Four spots? Solid gold-mine.) As I was getting out of my car, an older guy in a suit walked past me, heading to his car, parked in the clergy spot next to mine.

As he walked by and saw me getting out, he stopped, did a visible double take, and took several deliberate steps backward, just so he could give me the stink-eye. It is worth mentioning that he was wearing a suit, on a 90-degree day, *and* carrying a Bible. Which tells me he is not only super-serious about Jesus, he is also super-serious about himself—and life in general. Meanwhile, I was climbing out of my car, wearing a backless yoga top (with appropriate tank top underneath) and my uniform Teva sandals. Because *one of our kids was sick,* and sometimes you just go. Looking serious or not.

Rev. Serious literally walked out of his way so he could give me a mean, judgy look—for being in a spot that he probably thought I had no right to. When I met his eye, he kind of shook his head sadly and walked away.

I could spend all day guessing at the nature of his disgust. Most likely, he figured I could not possibly be a minister and was hijacking a parking space that was not mine for the taking. Maybe he realized I *was* clergy, and that bothered him even more. Maybe he was scandalized, regardless, by what I was wearing. I will never know. But he was clearly bothered by my very existence in that moment and questioned my right to be where he was.

Some former version of myself would have just inwardly seethed and gone about my business. But nossir. I was not having this today. I was up to my inappropriate neckline in the history and culture of patriarchy, and he was not going to walk away that easily.

I walked around the back of my car, in my above-the-knee skirt, and I looked right at him and said, "Do you need to see some ID?"

He seemed flabbergasted that I was addressing him. Directly.

"Wha—what?" he stammered.

"I said," I laughed this time, having been super-serious before, "Do you need to see some ID?"

"I was just curious," he muttered awkwardly. "Well, I've got it if you need it," I shot back. He got into his car as quickly as his ill-fitting suit would allow him.

You do not mess with a woman on a mission.

My mission, in that moment, was to go comfort a sick kid *and* smash the patriarchy. I can do both. We contain multitudes, right?[1]

I can be an occasional yogi, an all-the-time pastor, and a barely-on-deadline writer. I can be gracious and compassionate, and I can also get kind of bitchy when I need to. I can rest in what is, and I can push boundaries. I can be a great cook and a terrible housekeeper. I can be the world's okayest mom and the most adequate wife on the block. I can throw out all my high heels and underwires and still wear mascara and cover my gray roots.

Because I am my own person, and I can do and be whatever I want. What I do *not* have to be is any of the things this man in the hospital parking lot thought I *should* be. I don't have to stay within any of the boundaries where he clearly thought I belonged; I don't have to be silent as he judges me; and I don't have to back down to the kinds of authority that men like him assume over women like me every day.

It was a fifteen-second exchange. Yet in so many ways it captured all the issues at the heart of this book. In that one moment, in one glance this man decided that I should not be there.

Maybe I should have asked *him* to show *me* his proper credentials. How do I know he's legit? Is the suit supposed to carry the title?

No. But the white maleness is.

This man's sense of entitlement to judge my fitness for that space is rooted solely in those two parts of his being—he is a white man, and that is supposed to be enough for anybody who's asking.

Well, I'm over that. I hope that, after reading this book, you are too. Men and women alike are going to have to start addressing and resisting judgments like this if we want to shift the balance for our daughters and our granddaughters.

While that parking-lot pastor has no real bearing on my life—I mean, he didn't have the authority to oust me from the parking space—he still carries a weight of authority. His misogynistic assumptions are upheld, after all, by the brand of gospel he must certainly preach at his church. And in that church, he probably does carry tremendous authority. He is preaching to people who are members of my community: people who are parents and teachers at our local schools, business leaders and employers, civic leaders and public servants, first responders and policy makers. Pastors like him, in shaping the worldview of people in all these spheres of public life, do in fact have a great deal of authority in creating the narrative in which we all have to live.

My concern is that not enough of us are working on creating the counter-narrative.

But my greatest hope is that we are beginning to find both the motivation and the language to do just that: to preach and embody and lead toward an ethic of equality that transcends the rhetoric of politics and pious sound bites. This season of political discourse has been some of the most toxic in American history, and in many ways it has brought out the absolute worst of how our country treats and envisions its women. But maybe it has also called out the best in us.

We women can't do it alone. We need men of good faith in our corner. We also need a narrative of faith that is life-giving for all, not just those who already hold the most cards.

We are living in a time in which women have more opportunity than ever before. We have female role models in any given field, however underrepresented we may be in some. We have at our fingertips technology and communication tools that our grandmothers never dreamed of. At least the letter of the law (if not its application) is working on our side. The future is wide open for women who want to be trailblazers toward whatever comes next. With more women than ever serving in pulpits, in government, and in the corporate world, maybe we can push this particular boulder the last few steps up the hill for those who came before us—and those who will come after.

While many of the justice issues for women take place in the secular world, the narrative that upholds that imbalance finds its greatest strength in organized religion. If we truly want to see women achieve equal status in our lifetime, the church must decide: Are we using the authority of the gospel to prop up the status quo? Or to transform the world? Is Scripture meant to be a weapon of control and manipulation? Or a story of freedom, empowerment, and fullness of life for all God's people?

In spite of everything, I still believe in the power of that story to liberate us all. It's all in the telling. And in how well we persist, together.

Notes

Chapter 1: The Patriarchy Dies Hard

1. Rodney Stark, *The Rise of Christianity* (Princeton, NJ: Princeton University Press, 1996), 10–12.
2. Laura Bates, *Everyday Sexism: The Project That Inspired a Worldwide Movement* (New York: Thomas Dunne Books, 2016), 60.
3. Ibid., 5.
4. Ibid., 17.
5. Susan Chira, "Why Women Aren't C.E.O.s, According to Women Who Almost Were," *New York Times*, July 21, 2017, https://www.nytimes.com/2017/07/21/sunday-review/women-ceos-glass-ceiling.html.
6. Ashley Emmert, "The State of Female Pastors," www.WomenLeaders.com, October 15, 2016, https://www.christianitytoday.com/women-leaders/2015/october/state-of-female-pastors.html.
7. Rachel Held Evans, "Who's Who among Biblical Women Leaders," www.rachelheldevans.com, June 6, 2012, https://www.rachelheldevans.com/blog/mutuality-women-leaders.
8. Galatians 3:28.

Chapter 2: Other Women Are Not the Problem

1. Nadia Abushanab Higgins, *Feminism: Reinventing the F-Word* (Minneapolis: Twenty-First Century Books, 2016), 16–24.
2. Ashley Parker, "Karen Pence Is the Vice President's 'Prayer Warrior,' Gut Check, and Shield," *Washington Post*, March 28, 2017, https://www.washingtonpost.com/politics/karen-pence-is-the-vice-presidents-prayer-warrior-gut-check-and-shield/2017/03/27/3d7a26ce-0a01-11e7-8884-96e6a6713f4b_story.html?utm_term=.b93fbbf5186b.

3. Emma Green, "How Mike Pence's Marriage Became Fodder for the Culture Wars," *The Atlantic*, March 30, 2017, https://www.theatlantic.com/politics/archive/2017/03/pence-wife-billy-graham-rule/521298/.

4. Tim Funk, "Mike Pence Follows 'Billy Graham Rule'—Created to Avoid 'Naked Lady with a Photographer'," *Charlotte Observer* April 4, 2017, http://www.charlotteobserver.com/living/religion/article 142611599.html.

5. Katie Rogers, "White Women Helped Elect Donald Trump," *New York Times*, November 9, 2016, https://www.nytimes.com/2016/12/01/us/politics/white-women-helped-elect-donald-trump.html.

Chapter 3: The Privilege Problem

1. Gail Collins, *When Everything Changed: The Amazing Journey of American Women from 1960 to the Present* (New York: Little, Brown and Co., 2009), 106–7.

2. bell hooks, *ain't i a woman* (New York: Routledge, 2015), 30–33.

3. Ibid., 28.

4. Barbara MacHaffie, *Her Story: Women in Christian Tradition* (Minneapolis: Fortress Press, 1989), 4.

5. hooks, *ain't i a woman*, 127.

6. Ibid., 137.

7. Ibid., 106.

8. Collins, *When Everything Changed*, 111.

9. Mosi Reeves, "Beyonce's 'Lemonade' Film Offers Stunning Visuals, Urgent Themes," *Rolling Stone*, April 24, 2016, https://www.rollingstone.com/music/news/beyonces-lemonade-film-offers-stunning-visuals-urgent-themes-20160424.

10. Ijeoma Oluo, via www.ijeomaoluo.com.

11. Matthew 15:21–28.

12. Jacqui Lewis, "Jesus Is Woke: We Should Be Too," *On Scripture*, August 20, 2017, https://www.onscripture.com/jesus-woke-we-should-be-too.

13. OnBeing Studios, *OnBeing* podcast with Krista Tippett, Ruby Sales, guest, September 15, 2016.

Chapter 4: Using Our Words

1. April DeConnick, *Holy Misogyny: Why the Sex and Gender Conflicts in the Early Church Still Matter* (New York: Continuum International Publishing Group, 2011).

2. Walter Brueggemann, *Genesis*, Interpretation: A Bible Commentary for Teaching and Preaching (Louisville, KY: John Knox Press, 1982).
3. DeConnick, *Holy Misogyny*, 5–6.
4. Ibid., 15–30.
5. Brueggemann, *Genesis*, 25.
6. Lisa Davison, "Just Language Covenant." Class notes, used with permission.
7. Barbara MacHaffie, *Her Story: Women in Christian Tradition* (Minneapolis: Fortress Press, 1989), 146–47.
8. Claire Cane Miller, "How to Raise a Feminist Son," *New York Times*, June 2, 2017, https:www.nytimes.com/2017/06/02/upshot/how -to-raise-a-feminist-son.html.

Chapter 5: The Motherhood Myth

1. Sarah Bessey, *Jesus Feminist: An Invitation to Revisit the Bible's View of Women* (New York: Howard Books, 2013), 126–27.
2. Phillip Cohen, "Fertility Trends and the Myths of Millennials," *Family Inequality* blog, February 20, 2017, https://familyinequality.word press.com/2017/02/20/fertility-trends-and-the-myth-of-millennials/.
3. George Gallup and Evan Hill, "The American Woman," *Saturday Evening Post*, December 22, 1962, http://www.unz.org/Pub/SatEvening Post-1962dec22-00015.
4. Gail Collins, *When Everything Changed: The Amazing Journey of American Women from 1960 to the Present* (New York: Little, Brown and Co., 2009), 55–56.
5. Alice Connor, *Fierce: Women of the Bible and Their Stories of Violence, Mercy, Bravery, Wisdom, Sex, and Salvation* (Minneapolis: Fortress Press, 2017), 42, 48.

Chapter 6: Equal Pay and Representation

1. Susan Chira, "The Universal Phenomenon of Men Interrupting Women," *New York Times*, June 14, 2017, https://www.nytimes .com/2017/06/14/business/women-sexism-work-huffington-kamala -harris.html.
2. Gail Collins, *When Everything Changed: The Amazing Journey of American Women from 1960 to the Present* (New York: Little, Brown and Co., 2009), 63–67.

3. Ibid., 74–76.

4. Ibid., 75–77.

5. Ibid., 81.

6. Jasmine C. Lee, "Trump's Cabinet So Far Is More White and Male Than Any First Cabinet since Reagan's," *New York Times,* March 10, 2017, https://www.nytimes.com/interactive/2017/01/13/us/politics/trump-cabinet-women-minorities.html.

7. Lucia Graves, "Why Are 13 Men In Charge of Healthcare for All American Women?," *Guardian,* June 28, 2017, https://www.theguardian.com/us-news/2017/jun/28/womens-healthcare-republican-senate-bill.

8. Just a nerdy Hamilton reference.

9. Ellen Bravo, *Taking On the Big Boys: Or Why Feminism Is Good for Families, Business, and the Nation* (New York: The Feminist Press, 2007), 24.

10. Ibid., 49.

11. Statistics are available via Department of Labor, www.dol.gov.

12. Statistics are available via National Women's Law Center, www.nwlc.org.

13. Nadia Abushanab Higgins, *Feminism: Reinventing the F-Word* (Minneapolis: Twenty-First Century Books, 2016), 36–37.

14. Marie Wilson, *Closing the Leadership Gap: Add Women, Change Everything,* rev. ed. (New York: Penguin Books, 2007), xiii–xiv.

15. Ibid., 29.

16. Ibid., xvii.

17. Emily Lund, "Minding the Gap: Gender and Compensation in Churches and Ministries," Church Law and Tax, March 28, 2017, https://www.churchlawandtax.com/web/2017/march/gap-gender-and-compensation-in-churches-ministry.html.

18. Wilson, *Closing the Leadership Gap*, 11.

Chapter 7: Stop Telling Me to Smile

1. Barbara MacHaffie, *Her Story: Women in Christian Tradition* (Minneapolis: Fortress Press, 1989), 10–11.

2. Ibid.

3. Ibid., 13.

4. Matthew 26:6–13; John 12:1–11; Luke 7:36–50.

5. April D. DeConick, *Holy Misogyny: Why the Sex and Gender Conflicts in the Early Church Still Matter* (New York: Continuum International Publishing Group, 2011), 143.

6. Ibid., 135.

7. Bené Viera quoted in Erika Hardison, "It's Important for Men to Understand That They Need to Stop Telling Women to Smile," *HuffPost Blogs*, April 11, 2016, https://www.huffingtonpost.com/erika-hardison/its-important-for-men-to-stop-telling-women-to-smile_b_9655246.html.

8. Eun Kyung Kim, "Kentucky Student Violates Dress Code with Exposed Collarbone," www.today.com, August 15, 2015, https://www.today.com/style/Kentucky-student-violates-high-school-dress-code-exposed-collarbone-t39211.

9. Jason Hancock, "Missouri Legislators Suggest Intern Dress Code, but Speaker Nixes the Idea," *Kansas City Star*, August 18, 2015, https://www.kansascity.com/news/local/news-columns-blogs/the-buzz/article31374875.html.

10. Lyndsey Matthews, "This School Just Adopted a Body-Positive Dress Code," *Cosmopolitan*, September 5, 2017, https:www.cosmopolitan.com/lifestyle/a12175310/body-positive-school-dress-code/.

Chapter 8: The New Frontier

1. Anna Silman, "A Timeline of Leslie Jones's Horrific Online Abuse," *The Cut*, August 24, 2016, https://www.thecut.com/2016/08/a-timeline-of-leslie-joness-horrific-online-abuse.html.

2. Lindy West, "Real Men Might Get Made Fun Of," *New York Times* online, July 12, 2017, https://www.nytimes.com/2017/07/12/opinion/real-men-might-get-made-fun-of.html.

3. OnBeing Studios, *OnBeing* podcast with Krista Tippett, Ruby Sales, guest, September 15, 2016.

Chapter 9: Domestic Abuse and Sexual Assault

1. Bill Chappell, "Montana Judge Is Publicly Censured over 30-Day Sentence for Rape," National Public Radio, July 22, 2014, https://www.npr.org/sections/thetwo-way/2014/07/22/334069164/montana-judge-is-publicly-censured-over-30-day-sentence-for-rape.

2. More statistics are available at www.endthebacklog.org.

3. Charlotte Alter, "Todd Akin Still Doesn't Get What's Wrong with Saying 'Legitimate Rape,'" *Time*, July 17, 2014, https://www.time.com/3001785/todd-akin-legitimate-rape-msnbc-child-of-rape/.

4. Gail Collins, *When Everything Changed: The Amazing Journey of American Women from 1960 to the Present* (New York: Little, Brown and Co., 2009), 321.

5. Statistics are available via www.RAINN.org.

6. Leora Tanenbaum, *I Am Not a Slut: Slut-Shaming in the Age of the Internet* (New York: HarperCollins, 2015), 243.

7. www.RAINN.org.

8. C. Shawn McGuffey, Boston University, personal correspondence, September 4, 2017.

Chapter 10: The Political Uterus and Hope of a Better Way

1. Laura Cox, "Viewers' Anger at 'Graphic' Call the Midwife Scene," *Daily Mail UK*, February 18, 2013, https://www.dailymail.co.uk/news/article-2280850/Call-Midwife-Viewers-anger-graphic-scene=backstreet=abortion.html.

2. Jason Motlagh and Suez Taylor, "This Is What a World without Reproductive Rights Would Be Like," *Marie Claire*, April 25, 2016, https://www.marieclaire.com/culture/news/a20069/abortion-outlaws-el-salvador/.

3. David Grimes and Linda G. Brandon, *Every Third Woman in America: How Legal Abortion Transformed Our Nation* (Carolina Beach, NC: Daymark Publishing, 2014).

4. More information about waiting periods, state regulations, and mandatory doctor/patient agreements is available at www.guttmacher.org.

5. Christina Cauterucci, "New Study: Anti-Abortion Laws Don't Reduce Abortion Rates. Contraception Does," Slate, May 11, 2016, https://www.slate.com/blogs/xx_factor/2016/05/11/abortion_rates_are-constant_in_developing_countries_while_developed_ones.html.

6. Trip Gabriel and Michael Luo, "A Born-Again Donald Trump? Believe it, Evangelical Leader Says," *New York Times*, June 25, 2016, https://www.nytimes.com/2016/06/26/us/politics/a-born-again-donald-trump-believe-it-evangelical-leader-says.html.

7. Camila Domonske, "Supreme Court Strikes Down Abortion Restrictions in Texas," National Public Radio, June 27, 2016, https://

www.npr.org/sections/thetwo-way/2016/06/27/483686616/supreme
-court-strikes-down-abortion-restrictions-in-texas.

8. Lorena O'Neil, "Meet the Pro-Life Millennials," *Marie Claire*, February 23, 2017, https://www.marieclaire.com/politics/a25265/feminist
-pro-life-millenials/.

9. Ibid.

10. Religious Coalition for Reproductive Choice, www.rcrc.org.

Conclusion

1. From Walt Whitman, "Song of Myself," in *Leaves of Grass* (New York: Barnes and Noble Books, 1993), 25.